To Blanche, Don, and Bonnie,
with whom I first experienced
what family means

To Judy, Chris, and Ben,
with whom I continue to share
the great adventure
of creating family

PARENTING WITH LOVE AND LAUGHTER

Finding God in Family Life

Jeffrey D. Jones

JOSSEY-BASS
A Wiley Imprint
www.josseybass.com

Published by Jossey-Bass
A Wiley Imprint
989 Market Street, San Francisco, CA 94103-1741   www.josseybass.com

Jossey-Bass books and products are available through most bookstores. To contact Jossey-Bass directly call our Customer Care Department within the U.S. at 800-956-7739, outside the U.S. at 317-572-3986 or fax 317-572-4002.

Jossey-Bass also publishes its books in a variety of electronic formats. Some content that appears in print may not be available in electronic books.

The scripture quotations contained herein are from:

The New Revised Standard Version of the Bible, copyright © 1989 by the Division of Christian Education of the National Council of the Churches of Christ in the United States of America. Used by permission. All rights reserved.

The HOLY BIBLE: New International Version, copyright © 1973, 1978, 1984. Used by permission of Zondervan Bible Publishers.

Library of Congress Cataloging-in-Publication Data

Jones, Jeffrey D.
   Parenting with love and laughter: finding God in family life /
   Jeffrey D. Jones.—1st ed.
      p. cm.
   Includes index.
   ISBN 0-7879-6425-5 (alk. paper)
      1. Parents—Religious life. 2. Family—Religious life. 3.
   Parenting—Religious aspects—Christianity. 4. Family—Religious
   aspects—Christianity. I. Title.
   BV4529 .J653 2002
   248.8'45—dc21   2002007179

FIRST EDITION
PB Printing   10 9 8 7 6 5 4 3 2 1

CONTENTS

Acknowledgments. vii

Introduction viii

Section One.   1
   Live What You Want to Teach.   1
   Forget Yourself.   6
   Prepare Your Children for an Unknown Future. 10
   Make a Home in Faith and Family. 14
   Practice Grace. 19

Section Two 23
   Cherish Memories. 23
   Nurture the Experience of God. 27
   Practice Hushness 31
   Call Forth Gifts 35
   Encourage Standing Alone 40

Section Three. 45
   Accept the Reality of Change. 45
   Grasp What Might Be. 49
   Let Faith Conquer Fear. 53
   Trust That God Will Work Things Out 57
   Remember Resurrection 62

Section Four. 66
   Seeing Life as a Gift 66
   Continuing to Claim and Use Your Gifts. 70
   Being Honest. 74
   Letting Hopeful Things Shape Living 79
   Remembering What It's Really All About 82

Section Five   86
    Taking a Stand.   86
    Giving Thanks When the Going Gets Tough   90
    Letting Children Teach   94
    Speaking Truth with Love and Laughter.   98
    Relying on God's Forgiving Love. 102

Section Six 106
    Know When to Lay Back. 106
    Learn to Let Go While Staying Connected 110
    Expect to Be Surprised. 114
    Cherish the Moment. 117
    Take a Break 120

Section Seven. 124
    Play Together 124
    Share the Richness of the Past 128
    Find a Symbol. 133
    Create Rituals of Sharing. 138
    Celebrate Times of True Communion 142

Appendix: Using This Book with Small Groups. 145

Indexes 153

ACKNOWLEDGMENTS

THIS BOOK WAS A LONG TIME IN COMING. THE FIRST PIECES OF WRITING that eventually led to this finished work were columns in a local semiweekly newspaper. "Periodic Pondering," as the column was called, appeared in 1992 and contained commentaries on a wide range of life experiences. Over the years, people kept saying that they appreciated these "ponderings," and so the columns accumulated. *Pitman Today* editor Amy Martin's continuing encouragement has been important over these years—as have her occasional phone calls reminding me that if I didn't get another "pondering" in soon, she'd have to change the column's name to "Very Infrequent Ponderings."

As the book idea began to develop, important insights came from Randy Frame. Without his creativity and knowledge, the transition from "columns" to "meditations" couldn't have happened.

Renee Colson Hudson and Jeff Woods both read the first-draft manuscript. Each provided important insights that helped shape the final draft. I deeply appreciate their willingness to spend the time reading and commenting simply because there was something about the concept I was working with that interested them.

Of course, my deepest appreciation goes to my family. Every preacher knows the problems that can occur when you begin to use your spouse and children as sermon illustrations. These stories took it one step further, as I shared about our family with people in our hometown and now with an even broader community. My deepest thanks go to Judy, Chris, and Ben for their willingness to share our life together with others—but most of all for being family for me.

INTRODUCTION

FAMILIES ARE A PART OF GOD'S PLAN FOR CREATION. AS PARENTS, WE play a vital role in that plan. Being a parent is one of the greatest challenges of life. In a sense, it is intensely personal because it is about who we are—our identity and our purpose; it determines how we live and spend our time. But it is also highly relational because it provides the most intimate relationships of our lives. Being a parent is also a calling from God. Like all callings from God, it does not come to everyone. But those who are called and respond find that it inevitably touches every aspect of their living and shapes their very being.

People of faith have long recognized the importance of parenting. In recent years we have added parenting skills classes to the more traditional ritual of infant dedication. Like the ancient rituals, these classes are a way to affirm the importance of the role of parents and provide the support of the community of faith for those who undertake this great responsibility. Part of the power of these experiences is that many of them take place in the context of a small group in which there could be genuine sharing, caring, and support.

We in the church have rightly said to parents, "We know that parenting is one of the most important things you will do in life. We want to help you, so here is a way to increase your skills so you can be a better parent." This is good. It provides practical, concrete, down-to-earth support. There is no doubt about it. I've led parenting classes, and I know the profound and positive impact they can have on both parents and families.

However, there is something else the church can and should be saying to parents. And perhaps we haven't said this as well or as often as we could. It is this: "We know that parenting is one of the most important things you will do in life. We want to help you, so we are inviting you to deepen and enrich your relationship with Jesus Christ, because that, in and of itself, will make you a better parent." This, too, will provide practical, concrete, down-to-earth support, but in a different way. The truth behind this claim is that as Christ lives more fully in us, we are able to live more fully for others. Our own passions, needs, hurts, and wants get in the way less often, and we are able to listen, respond, and love more fully.

This book is written in the belief that the depth of our relationship with Christ profoundly impacts the quality of our parenting. It doesn't make great claims of transforming you as a parent. What it does is offer you an opportunity to reflect on your own family and your role in it from the perspective of faith: How is God at work? What is God trying to say to me? How can I make faith a more vital part of my experience as a parent and our experience as a family? This certainly isn't all that's needed to deepen your relationship with Christ, but it can be a part of it. When we can see God at work in the everyday events of life, when we see Christ in other people, adult and child alike, when we have confidence in God's love and constant care, our role as parents is transformed.

ABOUT THE BOOK

This book is written in the style of a conversation about families and parenting. In it, I have an opportunity to converse with you. Through it, you have an opportunity to converse with yourself and with God. The stories I tell about my family will help you to understand my faith perspective, but the real value for you will come as you delve into your own experience as a parent seeking to gain deeper understanding of its faith dimension.

The book is divided into seven sections, each providing five opportunities for conversation, each exploring a different insight about parenting. It does this in three ways: (1) a brief introduction, including a Scripture passage, that describes the insight and grounds it in the biblical passage; (2) a story from my own family that illustrates the insight; and (3) several questions to guide you in your own reflection.

The Bible passages are used not so much for formal Bible study as for a point of reflection. They have been selected because in them the writer seems to be dealing with a concern similar to that of the session. As you read a passage, take time to reflect upon it. I share some insights that it brings to the issue at hand, but Scripture speaks to different people in different ways. Take time to consider how God is speaking directly to you through each passage.

The conversations in each section are based upon a common theme:

✦ Section One takes a wide view, exploring the difference that a faith perspective can make in our families.

✦ Section Two offers some suggestions of hopes that can shape our parenting.

✦ Section Three takes a look at a range of things that we as parents have little control over and how faith helps us to deal with them.

✦ Sections Four and Five explore some of the more significant challenges we face as parents.

✦ Sections Six and Seven offer more specific suggestions for enhancing the faith dimension of our family life.

Each section is intended to provide material for a week of study and reflection. Recognizing the sometimes hectic pace of family life, I've included only five conversations for seven days. There will be days when you forget or simply don't have the time.

Although written primarily for parents, many of the stories and reflection questions lend themselves to use by families with older children and youth. I encourage you to share stories that have a particular impact or that touch on an issue that is important in your family. Use these stories as a way to begin a conversation within your family.

The appendix offers simple designs for a group to use to share the individual experience of each week, along with suggestions for an introductory session. Invite other parents to join you in using this book. Being able to share new insights and ongoing struggles will provide an extra dimension to this experience. All you need to do to form such a group is simply announce to others that this is what you would like to do, and invite any who share the same interest to join you. You might also speak personally to a few people you believe have the interest and with whom you'd like to share this experience. It's as simple as that! Those whose interest is deep enough to carry them through the seven weeks will respond. Those who don't respond in all likelihood do not have the necessary interest to keep going.

In order to create a comfortable environment for sharing, hold the weekly group sessions in a home. The host might serve light refreshments, but keep it simple. The focus of these meetings should be the sharing of the experiences and learnings of the week. The initiator of the group is often the one expected to lead. If that person is you, be willing to assume this responsibility, but also suggest taking turns and encourage others to take leadership each week.

MY OWN FAMILY

The stories that are told in each conversation are from my own experiences as a parent. They were written over a period of about ten years. Some were written shortly after the experience happened; others provide reflection on events that occurred many years earlier. In all of them, however, I explore what God might have been up to in the experience—how God was at work, what God might have been trying to tell me, ways in which God's love was revealed. They are, in a sense, journal entries about the experiences of my family and my experiences as a parent. Since the stories are used to illustrate the theme, they do not appear in chronological order. Each story is dated, however, so that you will know when it was written. Writing them proved to be my way of trying to see more deeply and understand more fully. My hope is that reading them will have a similar impact on you.

Since the stories are highly personal, let me take time before we begin to introduce my family. There are four of us: my wife, Judy; and our two sons, Chris and Ben; and me. Judy and I were married in 1975. Chris was born in 1980, Ben in 1983. As I complete the writing of this book, Chris has finished his junior year of college, and Ben has just graduated from high school, with plans to join Chris at the same college in the fall. During the time the stories were written, we've lived in a small town in southern New Jersey, just outside of Philadelphia. Most of that time I was the pastor of the American Baptist church in town. In 1998, I began a new job in the American Baptist Churches Mission Center, about an hour away. My daily commute has provided a regular time of thinking and prayer. This "forced" time of reflection has led me to probe even more deeply into the faith dimension of my life and family, and eventually led to the idea for sharing our experiences with others.

These are the basic facts about my family. They seem, as I reread them, rather cold. The warmth of the life we share together will become apparent in the stories that follow.

Let's begin!

SECTION ONE

I BELIEVE THAT ONLY THROUGH A LIVING, VITAL, DYNAMIC RELATIONSHIP *with Christ can we be the parents our children really need. Just learning the skills of parenting isn't enough. When Christ lives in you, you can take being a parent to a deeper level because Christ empowers you to:*

+ **Live What You Want to Teach**
+ **Forget Yourself**
+ **Prepare Your Children for an Unknown Future**
+ **Make a Home in Faith and Family**
+ **Practice Grace**

LIVE WHAT YOU WANT TO TEACH
Train children in the right way, and when old, they will not stray. (Proverbs 22:6)

In the broadest sense, what parenting is really all about is meeting the challenge to "train children in the right way." This involves much more than teaching the dos and don'ts of proper behavior. It's also about the values we live by, the faith we hold, the perspective we take on life. It's even about where we look to find meaning in life and in what happens to us. All of these things impact the way we and our children live. We teach these things, of course, in what we tell our children. Telling is important, because it makes the values, meanings, and perspectives

1

conscious. Beyond that, however, we also teach them in the way we live. This is the most powerful teacher. It is what gives the words power and makes them real. The way we live offers a more powerful message than words. Often, children see and understand more than we realize. Sometimes what they learn from the way we live is subconscious. At other times, however, they surprise us by putting the words to our actions and helping us to see what we have been teaching all along. It is these times that remind us what a powerful teacher our own lives are and why having Christ at their center is so important.

A Scary Thing   March 2000

Ben has an ability to raise interesting and sometimes difficult questions, especially when dealing with authority. This has provided one of the intriguing challenges involved in being his father. This trait of his surfaces both at home and in school on a fairly regular basis. Ben has never sparked a major controversy, but his teachers and the school administrators have learned that he is someone who won't simply roll over and play dead when his sense of what is right has been violated.

We've been going through one of these episodes of late. This one has to do with the National Honor Society, of which Ben recently became a member. It seems that he sees it as somewhat of an elitist organization that isn't sensitive to those on the "outside," especially those who are academically eligible but not selected for membership. This came to a head at the induction ceremony, in which the new inductees were instructed to talk about working for change in the world. Many talked about the way in which they would like to make the world a better place to live. Ben hit much closer to home. He talked about the need for change in the National Honor Society itself. I'm sure he ruffled a few feathers in doing this, but from my perspective he did it in a very responsible way. On top of that, I appreciated his real sensitivity to those who were feeling excluded. Besides, I had been the object of this special trait of his often enough that it was good to see someone else in the hot seat for a change!

We were talking about all of this one night at dinner, when suddenly Ben said, "This is kind of scary, Dad, but I'm starting to be a lot like you."

Apparently, in his eyes I am also one who asks the difficult questions, who tends to see things differently from most people, and who isn't afraid to let others know where I stand. I'd never thought about it quite that way before, but I guess he's right. Perhaps this *is* something he learned from me. Perhaps, in some perverse twist of fate, I am actually the one responsible for this quality that makes parenting him such a great adventure!

It's interesting, amazing, and a bit scary to see how much our children learn from us, even when we're not intentionally teaching—sometimes when we're not even aware of what we're teaching. The truth is that much teaching occurs just through being who we are as we relate to them. The longer I live and the more I grow as a parent, the more I understand that the thing that matters most is not what I've learned from books or workshops. Parenting doesn't depend on what knowledge I've acquired or what skills I developed. What matters most depends almost completely on who I am—at the very core of my being. That essence of me determines how I respond to the experiences and the people I encounter, how I live in those times when I'm not consciously planning what I will do or what I will say. My effectiveness as a parent depends a whole lot more on who I am than what I know.

That's why a deep and growing relationship with Christ is so vital to good parenting. Without that, we are too much into ourselves, too governed by our own needs, too insecure to step outside ourselves so that we can be for someone else. With this relationship, however, there is a power present in us that allows us to forget ourselves and live for others. There is a humility that lets us understand and accept who we are, warts and all. There is a confidence that comes from knowing we are loved. There is a sense of justice that comes from knowing how much God loves all people.

I've come to understand that these things are possible only as I open myself up to let Christ live more fully in me. When I do that, it's a joy to think of my sons becoming a lot like me.

Questions for Reflection

1. *What traits of yours did your children receive?*

2. *Have you ever come face to face with yourself in something your children have said or done? How did they learn that?*

3. *What qualities, characteristics, or personal traits of yours do you want to see appear in your children?*

4. *For you, what is the most important "content" in what you teach your children?*

5. *How does your relationship with Christ enhance your ability to teach this content?*

FORGET YOURSELF

"If any want to become my followers, let them deny themselves and take up their cross and follow me."
(Mark 8:34)

We live in an age that stresses the importance of self-fulfillment. Sometimes it becomes self-gratification. This focus on self can have a positive dimension to it. We are, after all, creatures created and loved by God, who are important to God, and who have legitimate needs to which we must attend. When overdone, however, self-fulfillment becomes a detriment to our families, and ironically enough, ultimately to ourselves. Jesus has an antidote to this danger. He talked about the need to deny ourselves, especially if we want to be his followers. I don't think he meant by this that we had to adopt some kind of self-sacrificing approach to relationships that turns us into little more than doormats. We've learned enough about codependence of late to know how unhealthy that is. Rather, Jesus was pointing us to the great truth that in the last analysis, serving others is how we find our true self and our greatest sense of self-fulfillment. It takes time and effort to learn how to live that truth. Part of it is learning when and how to set aside the things we are attending to in order to focus our attention on the things that matter to others.

The Wonder of Saying Yes   *September 1997*

Ben loves projects. I've never known anyone else who can become immersed so completely and intensely in something of interest. At one point it was the bass guitar; another time it was painting his room. No matter what the focus, however, there usually comes a point at which he needs me to be part of whatever it is he's doing.

A while ago the focus of his attention and energy was his bicycle. He was busy at work in the backyard changing a tire. I was busy at work in my study writing a sermon. He finished, and needed a ride to the gas station to fill the tire with air. I was still writing and didn't want to go anywhere. Being a dutiful father, however, I agreed to provide the needed ride. But in all honesty, I probably did it in a way that let him know that the interruption was not appreciated. The whole thing took about ten minutes. I was back in the study, working away, thankful that at last I might now have some peace and quiet.

It wasn't more than five minutes before Ben appeared once again. Sheepishly he explained that he had put the tire on incorrectly and that the only way to correct the mistake was to deflate the tire, remount it, and have me take him to the gas station again to reinflate it. Imagine the courage it took for him to say that!

I was annoyed, and, by my way of thinking, I had every right to be. I had important work to do; after all, sermon writing is my job—and it's God's work! I had already made one trip to the gas station, why should I make another? If he had done his work carefully in the first place, there would be no need to do it over. Imagine the things I might have said to him!

Through some wonder of the grace of God, however, what I did say was this: "That's okay, Ben. Sometimes I don't get things right the first time either." And off to the gas station we went.

Jesus talks about the need for us to deny ourselves if we want to follow him. That sounds like a horribly difficult thing to do. Sometimes it is. But sometimes it's as simple as saying yes to your children.

Questions for Reflection

1. *What are the interruptions you face from your children? What do you feel when they come to you? How do you usually respond?*

2. *Describe a time in which you handled an interruption well. What made this possible?*

3. *What would it take for you to view the interruptions as a natural part of your day, or even as an opportunity to show a special kind of love to your children?*

4. *In what other ways is it important to "deny yourself" in your relationship with your children?*

5. *How do you strike a balance between this and your own need to attend to yourself and other responsibilities?*

PREPARE YOUR CHILDREN FOR AN UNKNOWN FUTURE

A voice cries out: "In the wilderness prepare the way of the LORD, *make straight in the desert a highway for our God." (Isaiah 40:3)*

Clearly, childhood is a time of preparation, and one of our primary responsibilities as parents is to prepare our children for an unknown future. For our children, developing the skills they need, the moral code that will ground them, the sense of identity that will give them confidence, and the relationships that will nurture them will go a long way in giving them what they need to face in a rapidly changing world. The payoff might not be until five or ten or fifteen years down the road, but the preparation needs to happen now. This is especially true of both their and our relationship with God. That relationship is what gets us through the various crises of parenting without undue damage to either our children or ourselves. It's also what our children need to get through all that life will throw at them in the years ahead. One of our greatest gifts to them, then, is the environment and encouragement that allow them to develop a faith in God that will go with them into the future. We all face a wilderness or two in life; but, when we've prepared the road ahead of time, we and our children will find it easier to connect with God and find that straight highway we need.

Just Three Seconds   *April 1998*

I've been thinking about Dan McMaster a lot these past few weeks. Dan is the one whose last-second heroics secured our high school's second straight Group One state basketball championship. With just thirteen seconds left in the game, he stole an in-bounds pass, drove to the basket, and, when the opponents were charged with goaltending, was credited with the game-winning basket. All it took was three seconds.

Dan is a senior. This is his first year as a starter. He's played steady ball all year, but hasn't attracted much attention. Baseball, not basketball, is his first love in sports. And yet it was Dan who seized the moment, Dan who figured out what the play would be, Dan who took the risk of moving out of position to intercept the pass, Dan who took the shot. All it took was three seconds on the clock.

But it really took a lot more time that that. It took years of practice to develop the skills. It took hours of sitting on the bench watching how the game is played. It took months of playing in order to know enough to anticipate what was going to happen and act before it did. There's a sense—overstated, to be sure, but still true—that everything Dan had ever done in basketball was preparation for those three seconds. Because of that preparation, when the time came, he could respond in a way that led to victory.

Life is like that, I think. Each of us is confronted many times with our own "three-second experiences." There are the three seconds we have to respond to the misbehavior of a child; the three seconds we have to say "I love you" or say nothing; the three seconds we have to affirm rather than complain or blame. There are the three seconds in which we are confronted with an ethical dilemma at work; the three seconds in which we learn we have a life threatening disease; the three seconds in which a loved one meets death and we are left alone. How we have prepared will determine how we respond. How we respond will determine victory or defeat.

For me, an essential part of that preparation is faith—not in the religious sense, but in the relationship sense. Faith in the sense of building a solid, secure relationship with God. A relationship that provokes us, prods us, and challenges us as much as it comforts us and gives us peace. A relationship that becomes so much a part of who we are and how we live that it really does shape how we respond to each three-second opportunity in life.

This kind of relationship does not happen overnight. It doesn't miraculously appear when the need is great, any more than Dan's insight and skill appeared at the thirteen-second mark of the championship game.

It takes time. It takes effort. It takes sticking with it even when it's tough, even when it doesn't seem to be producing much in the way of great results. But when the time comes, it's there, to be called on, to shape what we will do, to help us respond in a way that brings victory. To my way of thinking, there is no better preparation for living.

Questions for Reflection
1. *What "three-second" experiences have you had in your life? As a parent?*

2. *In what ways did something you had learned before help you through those experiences?*

3. *Did you draw on your relationship with God in those "three-second" experiences? If so, in what ways?*

4. *What can you do now to better prepare both yourself and your children for life's "three-second" experiences by deepening your relationship with God?*

MAKE A HOME IN FAITH AND FAMILY

And you shall hallow the fiftieth year and you shall proclaim liberty throughout the land to all its inhabitants. It shall be a jubilee for you: you shall return, every one of you, to your property and every one of you to your family. (Leviticus 25:10)

We all need a place to belong, a place that's home for us. We can get lost so easily. In today's world it happens so often and in so many ways that it's easy to find ourselves without a place to call home, and we're left wondering how it all happened.

That is what happened to the prodigal son in Jesus' famous parable in Luke 15. The same theme is found well back into the Old Testament. This ancient idea is as meaningful today as it was thousands of years ago. One Old Testament solution for the problem was the year of Jubilee. Every fifty years there would be a time of return—a time to set things right that had gone wrong, a time to return to the places and people of our grounding. So, slaves were freed, debts were forgiven, and people returned home to be in the place where, and with the people with whom, they could begin again. What great wisdom! It acknowledges the great truth that in order to live in a world that pulls us in so many ways, we need at least one place where we can get back to our roots—to what matters most—to be reconnected to what life is really all about.

That is what a family can be. Sure, demands are placed on families too—demands that pull us in many ways. Sometimes it may seem impossible to set all that aside. And yet, our families remain important places of grounding for us in life. That is especially true if our families themselves are grounded in faith.

Grounded   *September 1999*

I've been traveling in New England this week. I always like coming back here. I grew up in Rhode Island, and deep down I'll always be a New Englander. I haven't lived here for almost thirty years now, but I'm still a Red Sox fan, and I brought my sons up to be Red Sox fans as well. Being a Red Sox fan, of course, involves a good deal of pain, but most good things in life have at least some pain associated with them.

As I traveled around New England, I couldn't help but think I had come home. That's a bit odd when you think about it, because I spent most of my time in Maine, New Hampshire, and Vermont—places I never really lived in. Still, it felt like home to me. There is, I think, a sense of being grounded there that gives a feeling of home. I can't describe it or explain it, but I know how it feels.

We all need that sense of grounding in our lives. The place that feels "right" to us—where we can let down our guard a bit, and where living seems to take less effort. I get that feeling, for some reason, whenever I'm in New England. I also get it when I'm with my family. Family is where I can be me and still be loved, a familiar place that I know and where I'm known. It's a place of grounding for me. Without that kind of place, it's impossible to function in a world that's often strange—where people don't really know me, where judgment comes easily, and everything seems to take a great deal of effort.

Faith is about grounding, too. It provides a foundation for living in what can often be difficult circumstances. It provides the "home" we all need to make life more than mere existence. For me, it gives a sense of grounding, the experience of being loved even though I'm known through and through, of being connected to what matters most. Just like when I travel to New England and it feels like home, I can't explain it but I know how it feels. And I know that it makes all the difference in the world.

Questions for Reflection

1. *Is there a place for you in which you feel a real sense of being at home, of being grounded? Describe it and what makes it so special for you.*

2. *In what ways does your family provide the same kind of feeling for you?*

3. *In what ways can you help your children develop that sense of being grounded in your family?*

4. *In what ways does faith provide a similar sense of grounding for you and your children?*

5. *What gets in the way of this grounding happening through family and faith? What helps it happen?*

PRACTICE GRACE

*For by the grace given to me I say to everyone among
you not to think of yourself more highly than you
ought to think, but to think with sober judgment,
each according to the measure of faith that God has
assigned. . . . Let love be genuine; hate what is evil,
hold fast to what is good; love one another with
mutual affection; outdo one another in showing
honor. (Romans 12:3,9-10)*

No matter how big they get, families begin with the relationship between two people. As the family grows, that relationship remains the foundation upon which the family builds. When that relationship is solid, the family can be strong. When it is not, the family struggles, as do those within it. There is a mystery to all of this that can never be completely unraveled. I am convinced, however, that what we learn in this relationship, what we are able to put into practice in it, has a great carryover into the wider family. In a sense, it might even be seen as a laboratory for working on intimate relationships, so that when children are added to the mix, we are more able to relate to them in positive and healthy ways. In writing to the church in Rome, Paul described the traits of Christian community. They are also the traits of the Christian family. In both places, such intimacy of relationship depends upon the presence of healthy doses of grace.

Twenty-five Years   *June 2000*
Judy and I celebrated our twenty-fifth wedding anniversary this week. From my point of view, we're both too young to be doing that. Actually, however, since we got a late start in married life, we're both older than the average silver-anniversary couple.

A lot has changed in those years. I've gained weight and gotten gray hair, as even a fleeting glance at our wedding pictures makes abundantly clear. Fashions have changed a good deal as well. What in the world ever possessed me to get a bright-blue tux with a ruffled shirt? Chris and Ben laugh uproariously when they see the pictures. I just cringe.

There have been more profound changes than these, however. We've moved around quite a bit. We met in Cincinnati, moved to Pennsylvania, then on to Rochester before settling in New Jersey. I've cycled through a number of jobs. Judy has become a full-fledged weaver, producing ever better woven wearables, winning prizes, and expanding her vision of who she might be.

Judy and I were a family of two back then. We've since become a family of four. We're fast on our way to being just two at home again. But no matter where they are, Chris and Ben will still be part of the family. This parenting thing is probably what's changed us the most. I can't even envision bringing new life into the world, nurturing it along through triumphs and struggles, and beginning to let it go without being profoundly affected by the whole thing. Along the way it radically changes the person you are because you've been tried and tested in ways you couldn't even imagine, you've seen great things about yourself that you didn't know were there before, and you've been confronted with other far less pleasant realities about yourself that you wanted to change as soon as you discovered them.

I've pondered a bit on how it is that we've made it this far. A lot of reasons come to mind. But the one that I keep coming back to is grace. That seems to be the best explanation. Part of it is the grace of God— that inexplicable something that surprisingly happens to you and leaves you wondering how and why you deserve it. Part of it is human grace, too. I know about the grace of Judy, because I know that I'm not always the easiest person in the world to live with. Almost always, I have a certain restlessness about me. Just look at the different places we've lived, the different jobs I've had. But it isn't just because of me that I know that grace had to be there. No two human beings could possibly live together for twenty-five years without grace being present in a powerful way—the grace to forgive, the grace to ignore, the grace to forget, the grace to keep quiet, the grace to simply accept.

Even that very human grace, however, brings us back to the grace of God. For I know from personal experience that God's grace at work in me is the only reason I am able to be gracious in my relationships with others. It's kept us going for twenty-five years, and God being God, it will for at least another twenty-five.

Questions for Reflection

1. *What special anniversaries has your family celebrated or will it be celebrating—not just weddings, but any kind?*

2. *How have these caused you to reflect on your life? What have you learned through that reflection?*

3. *When and how have you experienced grace in your family life—the grace to forgive, the grace to ignore, the grace to forget, the grace to keep quiet, the grace to simply accept?*

4. *How might you become more gracious in your relationships with others?*

SECTION TWO

*T*HE YEARS OUR CHILDREN ARE WITH US ARE YEARS OF PREPARATION *for the life they will lead without us. It's important to think about what we want to have happen in these years, to name our hopes so that we can live to bring them to reality. Some of my hopes for these years have been to:*

+ **Cherish Memories**
+ **Nurture the Experience of God**
+ **Practice Hushness**
+ **Call Forth Gifts**
+ **Encourage Standing Alone**

CHERISH MEMORIES
Therefore, since we are surrounded by so great a cloud of witnesses, let us also lay aside every weight and the sin that clings so closely, and let us run with perseverance the race that is set before us, looking to Jesus the pioneer and perfecter of our faith. (Hebrews 12:1-2)

Strength and confidence aren't always easy to come by. At times, life is difficult and painful. When our resources are exhausted and we have no reason to believe in our ability to get by any longer, feeling strong is difficult. And yet, the Bible says that God is the source of strength for us, a strength that is available to us at all times, even in the midst of great sadness, when we are feeling weak and vulnerable. The memories we have of those who are important to us provide one important source of that strength for us. That is what the author of Hebrews was referring to when he wrote about "the great cloud of witnesses" that surrounds us. The example they set, the model they offer, provide strength and confidence. This is what allows us to keep running the race that is set before us. And as we run, we become aware of the real source of confidence, both for them and ourselves. It is, of course, Jesus. Real confidence and strength comes from the faith that Christ is there in the midst of it all. Christ knows what it's like for us as we run the race. Christ has been there. Christ is there—supporting, caring, uplifting, even crying along with us if that is what we are doing. In the last analysis, that is the best and greatest reason for confidence in our lives. When we bring this attitude to our family life, it makes the tough times easier. It provides a special way of seeing that is a precious gift to our children.

The Wonder of Baseball   *October 1999*

Tears came to my eyes when they introduced Ted Williams before the second game of the World Series the other night. I've always liked Ted Williams, but I couldn't figure out why seeing him there would have that kind of impact on me. Then I realized that it wasn't Ted Williams at all.

It was the times when I was a kid that my father took me to Fenway Park and we sat in the left-field seats and watched Ted Williams play.

It was the times my father and I played catch in our backyard.

It was the laughter and conversation my family shared around the dinner table each night as I was growing up.

It was the confidence about life that I sensed just because I knew my father was there and could always be relied on.

It was the faith I grew in because he and the rest of my family went to church each Sunday and he practiced what we learned there every day.

It was the joy I felt as a young man when I told my father that Judy and I were engaged to be married.

It was the pride I felt when I introduced him to his two grandsons, Chris and Ben.

It was the inexpressible thanks I've felt more than once when his generosity has made it possible for me and my family to do things that otherwise wouldn't have been possible.

It was the sense of continuity in life I experienced when he and I walked together to Chris's high school graduation.

It was the overwhelming gratitude I felt last summer when I stood beside his hospital bed after he had a stroke, and the doctors didn't know if he would make through the night, and I said, "Thanks for being such a great father."

It was the sense of determination and strength I saw as I took him to physical therapy last month and witnessed his amazing comeback from the effects of that stroke.

It was everything I felt about him, about life, as I pushed him in his wheelchair last week when our family visited him again and I thought about all these things.

Tears came to my eyes when they introduced Ted Williams the other night.

No wonder.

Questions for Reflection

1. *Describe one member of your family or extended family. List important memories you have of that person and the impact he or she has had on your life.*

2. *In what ways can these memories provide you with strength and confidence in difficult times?*

3. *How can you help provide these kinds of memories for your children?*

4. *Does an ongoing awareness of God being with you provide a sense of confidence in your life? If so, in what ways? If not, how can you increase this awareness of God's presence in your life?*

NURTURE THE EXPERIENCE OF GOD

Make me to know your ways, O LORD;
teach me your paths.
Lead me in your truth, and teach me,
for you are the God of my salvation;
for you I wait all day long.
—Psalm 25:4-5

I suppose that a case can be made that when it comes right down to it, the psalmist in these verses gives as good a brief statement of the purpose of faith as there is. All the fine points of theology aside, what really matters is walking in the paths that God intends for us. A whole array of things is required in order to do that, including a vital faith and a deep relationship with Christ, but that is where it all leads. That simple insight is an important one to share with our children. And yet, it is also one that is easy to forget.

Good, religious people, through no fault of their own, really, have a tendency to focus on concerns about correct biblical interpretation rather than on the way in which the Bible speaks to people. Similarly, they easily stray into thinking that knowledge about God is more important than the experience of God. I'm guilty of that. Thankfully, every now and then God provides a reminder that gets me focused correctly and helps me be more effective in sharing real faith with my children.

A Friend's Wedding   *May 2000*

A friend of mine got married last weekend. I haven't been able to say that in quite some time. I've long passed that point in life when it's one friend's wedding after another. And yet, it's true: a friend of mine got married last weekend.

Scott is a friend because we carpooled together for about two years. At two hours a day—allowing for business trips, vacations, and the like—I figure that that amounts to something like five to six hundred hours we've spent together with little to do but talk. That will either make or break a friendship. In our case, it made it. There's little else that would have brought us together otherwise. I've got about twenty-five years on him—old enough to be his father. Our political views aren't particularly compatible. Our interests, skills, and areas of work don't have much in common. But over the course of the past two years, a genuine friendship has developed. We've counseled and consoled each other. We've each listened as the other vented after a particularly difficult day at the office. He's been with me through some tough decisions I had to make. I've been with him through a series of new job opportunities that has come his way.

We do, however, have one very important thing in common: faith and a real desire to have faith shape our lives. I'm not talking about theology here, or doctrine, or anything like that. Scott and I probably have more differences than similarities on that count too. What I am talking about is faith—the basic belief that God is, that God has created each of us for some special reason, that God is at work in our lives to make that reason apparent to us so that we can begin to live up to God's intentions for us. The kind of faith the psalmist had in mind when he prayed, "Teach me your paths. Lead me in your truth." That is something Scott and I do have in common. And what I've learned from my friendship with him is that this is probably what matters most. It is certainly more important than doctrine. What really counts is the experience of God in our lives and our desire to deepen that experience so we can attune ourselves more fully to God's intentions for us. If we share that with others, it becomes an abiding common bond for relationship, both within the family and outside of it.

Questions for Reflection

1. *Who are the people in your life outside your church and family with whom you share about your faith? What is your relationship with them like?*

2. *What are the benefits of approaching life with "the basic belief that God is, that God has created each of us for some special reason, that God is at work in our lives to make that reason apparent to us so that we can begin to live up to God's intentions for us"?*

3. *How can the notion "What matters is the experience of God in our lives and our desire to deepen that experience so we can attune ourselves more fully to God's intentions for us" shape the way you nurture your children in faith?*

PRACTICE HUSHNESS
Better is a handful with quiet than two handfuls with
toil, and a chasing after wind. (Ecclesiastes 4:6)

In the effort to be better parents, we easily get caught up in the great concern of what we should, could, or might do. Almost always, we face the questions of what we need to do, say, or be in order to be most effective as a parent. Those are important questions. Answering them will greatly enhance our relationships with our children. There's no doubt about that. But another important truth stands in the midst of all of this for us. The writer of Ecclesiastes understood it. There are times when we simply have to put aside the wondering about what to do, say, or be. There are times when we simply need to be quiet and practice "hushness." Sometimes out of these times will come new insights or a new sense of relationship with God. Sometimes they will produce absolutely nothing. That's okay. What we are dealing with here is that essential corner of our lives in which productivity doesn't matter at all. It is that place where we simply exist, and know that is good enough. As parents, we need to seek out those times and places, because they usually do not present themselves. We rarely find ourselves in a situation in which we can say to ourselves, "Well, I have nothing to do for awhile, I think I'll have a handful of quiet now." In the excitement of new ventures, in the busyness of old routines, we must find the place and space where doing, saying, and being something does not matter.

A Special Day   *September 1998*
September 8 will live on as a special day in my memory. It was my first son's first day of classes at college. It was my first day in a new job.

Chris's first day of college came at the end of a long and at times difficult process of deciding, applying, waiting, being accepted and rejected, and committing. It involved moving 450 miles away and reestablishing himself with new friends in a new place. It meant, at least for his parents, a difficult goodbye and letting go. And yet, it was something for which all of us had planned and hoped for years.

My first day in a new job came quickly, even unexpectedly. I had, after all, just started another new job five months earlier. I was happy with what I was doing and very content with the lifestyle it enabled. I wasn't seeking anything, didn't apply for anything, did not have to worry about being rejected. It just happened. Deciding whether to say yes or no, however, took some thought. The change in work habits would be significant. But in the end, I, like Chris, said yes, and began a new adventure.

On this memorable day I drove to work by myself, listening to a tape of some old youth conference songs. One of them, written by a friend of mine, goes like this: "Hush now in quiet peace. Be still, your mind at ease. The Spirit brings release, so wait upon the Lord." It's the song I sang to rock Chris to sleep when he was a baby. It was what helped this rather intense young boy to relax, and fall restfully asleep in my arms.

It all seems to have happened too fast. One day, a restless baby in my arms; the next, an eager college student out on his own. One day, an inexperienced, concerned dad; the next, an experienced but no less concerned father.

And yet, the song and its words remain. It was and is my prayer for Chris. As he goes off into a life and world filled with new experiences that will excite him, scare him, challenge him, and threaten him, I hope he will still find time for quiet and hushness. It is my prayer for myself as well, even as it was years ago when I was tired and overwhelmed by the challenge of being a father. In fact, it is my prayer for everyone. All of us need these times. Such times may, in fact, be the only thing that will make it possible for us to keep going.

We all know about the speed with which life passes by. We all know the turmoil of change, whether it is planned or unplanned. We all know about the challenges and crises involved in being parents. We all have memories to cherish, present moments to challenge, futures that are unknown. We all need a word of comfort and assurance: "Hush now. . . . Be still. . . . The Spirit brings release, so wait upon the Lord."

Questions for Reflection

1. *What are the times of quiet in your life?*

2. *When did you last experience hushness with God? What prompted it?*

3. *In what ways does or could your own practice of hushness enhance your relationship with God?*

4. *In what ways does or could your own practice of hushness enhance your relationships as a parent?*

5. *How do you help your children find times of quiet in their lives, times when they can wait upon the Lord?*

Related Activity

Schedule a time and place to practice hushness. It might not be every-day; it may be once a week, or even less often. Look for ways to experience it on the drive to work, in a leisurely bath, on a walk in a park or in your neighborhood, or simply by turning off the television or stereo when you are alone.

CALL FORTH GIFTS

For this reason I remind you to fan into flame the gift of God, which is in you through the laying on of my hands. (2 Timothy 1:6, NIV)

Gifts are wondrous things. There are, of course, the gifts that make birthdays special and exciting days. There are the talents we have that from the perspective of faith are gifts from God. There are the spiritual gifts that Paul wrote so much about because they were the cause of both great deeds and great conflict in the early church. There's also another kind of gift that fascinates me. These gifts also come from God and are a part of us, but they're not talents. They are more like "qualities of being." They are so much a part of us, in fact, that we tend not to think much about them at all. They're just who we are. In order to discover these gifts, we usually need someone else—someone who sees them in us and knows enough to recognize that not everyone possesses them. These are the gifts that families can be really good at calling forth. It takes genuine intimacy to recognize these gifts and to trust someone enough to believe them when they tell you that you have one.

Although not father and son, Paul and Timothy had that kind of intimate relationship. And so, Paul encouraged Timothy in the use of the gift that Paul had originally helped call forth. It is what another person does that puts us in touch with the gifts within us. Although it may be up to us to develop and begin to use them, someone else still needs to be there to encourage us, to remind us of the gifts when we forget. This calling forth and nurturing of gifts is one of the most important roles we parents play in the lives of our children. It's a long and slow process. At times, no one even notices what's going on. But when our children's gifts have been recognized and developed, they are on the road to becoming the people God truly created them to be.

Not Another Pavarotti   *July 1997*

I am tempted to blame Miss Sutton. She was my third-grade teacher. She's the one who stood next to my desk during music. She's the one who heard me sing in a different way and criticized me for fooling around. She's the one who embarrassed me in front of the entire class. She's the one who started the tape that's been running inside me ever since. "I have a lousy voice. I can't carry a tune. I can't sing on key."

It's taken more than twenty years, but I'm finally beginning to learn that Miss Sutton was wrong. I *can* carry a tune. I *can* sing on key. My voice, while not quite as good as Pavarotti's, isn't really all that bad.

I've learned that that "different way" I was singing in third grade is something called "singer's formant." You do it by lowering your larynx, resulting in more resonance in your voice. Not everyone can do it. I can. Not only that, when I sing that way, I do better at carrying a tune and staying on key. I also have better range. When I sing that way, I sound different enough that my kids laugh. But I can't fault them. If Miss Sutton didn't know any better, I shouldn't expect it of them.

The end result of all this is that I am starting to enjoy singing. People might pull up to me at a stoplight and think I'm in agitated conversation with a nonexistent person. But I'm just singing. It's a lot of fun. I'm just sorry I had to wait until I was fifty to begin to enjoy it.

The Bible talks about the different gifts God has given us. Some of them are talents, like singing, others are things like empathy or intuition or the ability to organize things and people in an orderly way. They're all part of the person God made us to be. We become the people God intends us to be by developing these gifts. But we need others to help us recognize them and to let us try using them.

Without others, our gifts will go underutilized, perhaps even unrecognized. God intended for me to sing, I think. It's taken too long for me to discover that, but I'm doing what I can to make up for it.

God also intended for us to help others recognize and develop their gifts. God intended for all of us to do that. That's the big lesson for me in all of this. Families are a great place in which that can happen. I see how fragile we can be, especially as children, how even a few comments can make a big difference. That awareness should make us very cautious about the criticism we offer as parents, very careful about the ways we motivate our children to grow. But the opportunity imbedded in all of this is a wondrous one. It is the challenge of helping a child of ours, a child of God, grow into the person God created him or her to be.

Questions for Reflection

1. *In what ways have you become aware of your gifts because someone else helped you discover and nurture them?*

2. *In what ways has the development of a gift in your life been stunted because of something someone else said or did?*

3. *What are some of the gifts or qualities of being that you see in your children?*

4. *What can you do to help them discover and develop them more fully?*

Related Activity
Schedule a time, either one-on-one or with the entire family, to talk about the special qualities you see in each other. Often, a simple game can begin this process. You might ask everyone to describe how a family member resembles, for instance, an animal or a color. A sentence completion, such as "I like you because . . ." or "What's special about you is. . . ," can also work.

ENCOURAGE STANDING ALONE
"Choose this day whom you will serve, . . . but as for me and my household, we will serve the LORD."
(Joshua 24:15)

One of the greatest gifts we can give our children is the strength to stand up for the things that are important to them, to do the things that really matter in life. I don't believe that this is something we can teach from a three-point lesson plan. Rather, it comes from the example we set, the modeling we provide over the years. In this way we teach not only that it is possible to buck the tide and stand up for what you believe in, but also we teach what the issues are about which we should be different from others. I think that is what Joshua was doing that day when he called on the people of Israel to decide whom they would worship and serve. Certainly, he was declaring for himself what was important, but also he was teaching his children that this was an issue about which it was important to be different, to stand alone if need be. We can't expect young children to consistently take stands that put them at odds with their peers or with authority figures in their lives. Nor can we expect them to do so around issues of grave significance. Every once in a while, however, we can expect to see signs that tell us whether or not the lesson is being absorbed.

The Independent   *November 1996*
Election season is here. Time for the candidates to make their cases and for the voters to decide. Time also for mock elections in schools.

Ben's middle school decided to have an election in which students would be able to consider the merits of the Clinton and Dole candidacies. I'm certain that it seemed like a good idea to the teachers—a chance to have a civics lesson taken from the newspaper headlines, an opportunity for students to get involved rather than just do "book learning." What they hadn't thought about, however, was Ben and his penchant for independent thinking.

The problem began when students were asked to register as either Republicans or Democrats. Ben and a friend wrote "Independent" on their registration forms. It wasn't quite an act of civil disobedience, but it didn't sit well with those who had organized the election. Eventually, it led to a teacher taking Ben and his friend from the classroom to tell them that they needed to make a choice between being a Republican or a Democrat, that they could not be Independents. This hallway confrontation didn't have its intended result, however. Both refused, even reminding the teacher that they had a Constitutional right to be Independents. I don't know what the teacher thought of this. I do know, however, that on the day of the great political debate, when Republicans and Democrats gathered in the school auditorium to listen as stand-in candidates presented their party's positions, Ben and his friend sat alone in the principal's office.

Ben has grown up in a home in which we teach respect for authority. It begins with the way we want Ben to treat us as his parents and extends to include other adults and his teachers. He also comes from a family that is not particularly known for causing trouble. Neither Judy nor I relish conflict. Chris's teachers have consistently seen him as a highly cooperative student. Ben has, for the most part, followed that pattern.

Ben has also grown up in a home in which we teach the importance of being able to think and act for yourself. We believe that's how children and youth withstand the peer pressure that can so easily lead them into unhealthy and harmful activity. We believe that's how as adults they will be able to maintain their integrity in a world of questionable values.

At times, these two characteristics seem to be at odds with one another. This was one of those times. As Ben gave daily reports of his exploits, I couldn't help but be somewhat taken aback by his response to his teacher and his unwillingness to go along with the plans that had been made. And yet, I also couldn't help but admire the strength of his conviction and his determination to hold his ground.

In the grand scheme of things, how he registered for a mock election in middle school isn't all that important. But what this experience is teaching him about his own character and what it means to take a stand even against authority figures may be one of the most important lessons of his life.

We live in a society that, despite frequently invoking God's name and talking about Jesus, conducts itself in a way that falls far short of the values of the gospel. When I wonder how my children will find the strength to live as faithful disciples in such a world, I can't help but take heart from Ben's independent thinking.

Questions for Reflection

1. *When have you taken a stand on something that made you different from most other people, or put you in opposition to those in authority? Have you told members of your family about this?*

2. *Have your children ever taken a stand that put them at odds with friends or teachers? How did you respond?*

3. *What are the ways that you as a family encourage both respect for authority and independent thinking in each other?*

4. *What are some of the ways that people who are disciples of Jesus should be different from others?*

Related Activity

Develop an "Independent Family Project." Determine some area of need in which you think most other people are not acting as you think Jesus wants us to act. Decide how you as a family can act differently from others by responding to this need in a positive way. Work together to make it happen.

SECTION THREE

BEING CLEAR ABOUT THE HOPES WE HAVE CAN HELP US IN OUR ROLE *as parents, but many times, things are simply beyond our control no matter how intentional we are. In those times, we can find in our relationship with Christ the strength to trust, the ability to wait. It is Christ in us that frees us to:*

+ **Accept the Reality of Change**
+ **Grasp What Might Be**
+ **Let Faith Conquer Fear**
+ **Trust That God Will Work Things Out**
+ **Remember Resurrection**

ACCEPT THE REALITY OF CHANGE

Save me, O God,
for the waters have come up to my neck.
I sink in deep mire,
where there is no foothold;
I have come into deep waters,
and the flood sweeps over me.
                    —*Psalm 69:1-2*

It's not a pretty picture: floodwaters sweeping over me, and no firm place to stand. I don't know about you, but some days, that's a pretty accurate picture of how I feel in the midst of all

45

the change taking place around me. Things that I've relied on for years are gone. Answers that have always been right are wrong. Ways that have always worked don't. It's no different when it comes to my role as a parent. In fact, it might be even more difficult, because here the concern is not just for me, but for my sons as well. How do I help them swim if I am drowning? How do I provide the foundation they need for faithful living if there is no foothold?

One of the traditional affirmations of faith is that God will provide for us in such times, that faith can be a solid rock upon which to stand when all else is shifting sand. The psalmist knew this to be true. The same psalm that began with words of desperation ends with these words of praise: "I will praise the name of God with a song; I will magnify him with thanksgiving. . . . For the Lord hears the needy, and does not despise his own that are in bonds" (Psalm 69:30,33).

It's a Different World   *January 2001*

Chris came home from school over Christmas break with a new significant relationship in his life. He met her last semester; she's a year behind him at college. I'm sure that the relationship was enhanced by the time their group spent traveling around China during their semester abroad. It wasn't long after he arrived home that the first phone call came. Then presents were exchanged through the mail. Of course, there was a pretty steady flow of e-mail messages. And the phone calls continued, back and forth all during Christmas break. It all seems very typical. But I continue to marvel at one aspect of the whole thing. You see, she lives in Tokyo. The mail, the e-mail, the phone calls were all going half way around the world!

That's just one of the things that has happened lately to reinforce for me what a different world we live in from the one I grew up in. I wouldn't have even thought about calling Tokyo on a regular basis, but for Chris it's as natural as calling a neighbor. In fact, for me, a girlfriend who lived in Kansas would have been a pretty amazing circumstance! But alas, as the saying goes, "We're not in Kansas anymore!" The world I grew up in is gone. My sons are more comfortable in the world we live in now than I am. It's simply changing too fast for many people who were born before 1980 to keep up with it. As much as I try to come to terms with this newness, I'm probably destined to live the rest of my life as an alien.

I can bemoan this reality, but that won't do any good. And I certainly can't do anything to hold back the tides of change. I simply have to find a way to live with it.

For me, it helps to see what others have done in similar situations. Believe it or not, there's an ancient story that really helps here. It's a period of time in Israel's history called the Exile. Following defeat at the hands of the Babylonians, a significant number of the leaders of the nation were transported out of Jerusalem and forced to live in Babylon. There was no temple—and the temple had been essential to their worship of God. Their families, in many cases, were left behind. The work they had done to support themselves was no longer available to them. Their homes were gone. The places and people that provided continuity and familiarity were nothing but memories. The land in which they now lived had a different culture, a different religion. They were nobodies there.

So there they were, having lost everything they depended upon to give meaning and stability to their life, work, and faith. (I can relate to that!) And yet, they got by. A couple of things were especially important. They had faith that God was with them and would provide for them. They created new ways to respond to new realities, such as developing a new understanding of worship because they no longer had their temple. In short, they found the courage to let go of the things they had depended on for so long, the creativity to develop and try new things, the faith to trust in God. This is not a formula to follow. But it is a pretty good set of guidelines for life in this new world, where so often we seem to be losing so much of what we depended on in the past.

I may be an alien in this new world, but that doesn't mean I'm lost and lonely, helpless and hopeless, mournful and moping. I, like them, can find the courage, the creativity, and the faith to survive—and maybe even to thrive. Let the phone calls to Tokyo continue!

Questions for Reflection

1. *What are the changes taking place in the world that impact you most strongly in your role as a parent? How do you deal with them?*

2. *How might the guidelines from the Exile (let go of old things, develop new things, trust God) help you in meeting these challenges?*

3. *What are the things you need to let go of? What are the new ways you need to embrace?*

GRASP WHAT MIGHT BE

I am about to do a new thing; now it springs forth, do you not perceive it? (Isaiah 43:19)

Wide-eyed anticipation is one of the joys of childhood. It's almost always there as Christmas approaches, but it can pop up any time. When it does, we parents need to recognize that the line between supportive encouragement and sour realism is pretty thin. Sure, we should teach the need for delayed gratification, but we don't need to dump cold water on our children's dreams of what might be. I've not taken a scientific survey, but my guess is that children see a lot more hopeful possibilities in life than we adults do. Perhaps we're more realistic, or maybe we're just jaded.

When you stack all of this up with a God who seems to be constantly doing something new and is almost invariably excited about it, it's hard not to think that maybe our children have something on us. Maybe they still have this deep and imaginative hopefulness that God has and undoubtedly created us with.

Maybe we've lost it somewhere along the way in the trials and tribulations of life. At any rate, as we guide our children through life—a life in which they are growing and experiencing new things at a fairly constant rate—a measure of wide-eyed anticipation might be good for us. It will certainly help them in their growing. It might even help us.

Intense Anticipation   *June 1998*

Chris just graduated from high school. This has been a time of great celebration for our family. His grandparents and aunt were in town. We had a party for friends and their families. Judy and I even added to the celebration by taking a few days of vacation all on our own.

Both in the rush of graduation activities and in the quiet of the days away I couldn't help but reflect a bit on what was going on. This is a time to be thankful for the educators who touched Chris's life—the teachers from whom he learned, the guidance counselor who worked with him through the arduous process of applying to colleges, the administrators whose vision and hard work have continued to make a high school diploma mean even more. Watching the graduation ceremony and the celebration that followed, I was also deeply thankful for his friends and all they have been for him since we moved to town six years ago.

During this time I've sensed in Chris and his friends something I'd call intense anticipation. This fall they'll be heading off to college. That's exciting. But in the final weeks of high school it became clear to all of them that they would be losing something as well. The friends who have meant so much won't be there any more. The place they've lived will become a place they visit on school vacations. The life that had become so familiar as to seem boring at times will be totally new. They can't help but be just a bit sad and scared.

None of it, however, discounts the excitement they have about the future. A whole new world lies before them, filled with experiences, opportunities, and challenges that they haven't even begun to imagine. This is where the intense anticipation comes in. It is looking to the future with a whole array of intense feelings—from sadness to hope, from fear to excitement, from reluctance to eagerness.

I can't help but contrast that to the way that I and many other adults so often approach our lives. It's not unusual to get up in the morning anticipating that this day will be like yesterday, and that every day for at least the next year or so will be the same. Sometimes we feel trapped; sometimes it's just that we're such creatures of habit that change is difficult to imagine. Maybe we're just too comfortable with the way things are.

What would it be like to add a little intense anticipation to the mix? Life certainly would be a bit more interesting, perhaps even exciting. And it might even lead to new experiences, opportunities, and challenges—even at our age! If only we could let go of what is enough to grasp what might be.

I believe that's the way God intended life to be. It is, after all, what being creative is all about, and we're made in the image of this creator God. It is also what newness is all about, and one of the consistent themes of the Bible is that God is the one who bring newness, sometimes even forces it on us.

If, like me, you sometimes wonder if this is all there is to life, if you wake up in the morning certain that this day will be just like any other day, if at times you feel that the groove you're in has become a rut, then why not try a little intense anticipation about what might be? It does wonders for high school graduates. It might just be the way life is supposed to be lived.

Questions for Reflection

1. *In what ways do you see a sense of excitement about the future in your children?*

2. How does this compare or contrast with the ways in which you anticipate the future?

3. What new possibilities might God be creating in your life that you haven't been able to see yet?

4. *What can you do to help your seeing?*

LET FAITH CONQUER FEAR

"Why are you afraid? Have you still no faith?"
(Mark 4:40)

I still remember the fear and uncertainty of the first time I held Chris in my arms. The joy was great, all but overwhelming. I felt a profound sense of awe and wonder. But still, there was the fear, the uncertainty about whether or not I could handle the great responsibility entrusted to me. Over the next several days and weeks the awe and wonder subsided, but the fear and uncertainty did not. Each day brought new challenges, new questions about my ability to be what I needed to be. With time, I learned I could do it. But then another new challenge would arise and the wondering would begin again. That's the way it has been ever since. I suppose I've grown more confident along the way. But the most important thing that has happened is that I've grown in faith— faith in myself as a father, faith in God as the one who will always be there, always keep me going. When Jesus saw fear in the disciples, he knew that what they really lacked was faith. The same kind of faith is what's needed for us to be good parents. Without it, the fears get to us and we do all sorts of crazy things that end up hurting our children, stunting their growth, making it more difficult for them to mature in faithful ways. With it, both they and we have freedom to become the people God created us to be.

On Uncertainty and Fear   *February 1999*

For the past three years my front hall has stood as a monument to my uncertainty and fear. It all began innocently enough. The woodwork in our house is chestnut, but over the years it had been covered with several coats of paint. Somehow it seemed wrong to have all that potential beauty hidden, so I set out to make it right.

The problem, I soon discovered, was that removing paint from the woodwork of three windows, three doors, and the accompanying baseboards is not easy. It's even more difficult when you don't know how to do it and have to keep experimenting before you come upon the considerably less than simple five-step process that actually works.

To that add cracking plaster that you don't know how to patch, and you've got even more experimenting—with a lot more error than trial. On top of that, I had the paradoxical misfortune of realizing that the patching I did manage to get done blended quite adequately with the existing white walls. That pretty much eliminated any aesthetic incentive to get the work done quickly!

At any rate, that was the state of affairs for more than three years. I'd work a bit, find it difficult, move on to other things, work a bit more, get frustrated, move on to other things, work a bit more, be unhappy with the results, move on to other things, work a bit more, ruin what I had already done, move on to other things, work a bit more. . . . You get the picture.

Finally, having promised the family that we would not have to decorate a stained and ugly staircase for the fourth Christmas in a row, I got the stripping finished just before Thanksgiving. Then we had a problem with color. What would we do with the walls? I did not want plain paint, but Judy didn't want wallpaper. I wanted something bold, but Judy feared that it would be too dark. Judy wanted it to coordinate with the rest of the first floor, but I have no sense of color at all.

So there it sat again, through Christmas on into the new year. Then we did try one thing, but both of us hated it. There it sat again. Finally, two weeks ago, we hit upon the right combination. Judy has completed the walls. I'm just now finishing the staircase. It will be done, completed, finished, you might even say consummated, within a matter of a week or two. And you know what? We really like it!

So now we can't help but wonder why in the world it took us so long, what it was we were so afraid of, why we were so uncertain of our ability to do it.

This just might be a parable about family life. Many times, uncertainty and fear hang us up, immobilize us, and make things just generally unpleasant. But often, it's not really as bad as it seems. The uncertainties are not as valid. The fears are not as potent. We get through it, and even more, we come out of it actually liking what has happened.

For the front hallway, faith in Judy and myself was enough. For being parents, faith needs to be in someone much bigger. I'm glad God is there with the courage and grace we need to get us through it!

Questions for Reflection

1. *When have you encountered a fear about your ability to be what you needed to be as a parent?*

2. *How did that fear immobilize you?*

3. *How did you get through it?*

4. *How does your faith in God help you to conquer the fears you have as a parent?*

TRUST THAT GOD WILL WORK THINGS OUT

We know that all things work together for good for those who love God, who are called according to his purpose. (Romans 8:28)

When it comes to our children, it's hard for us not to try to make things right for them—to fix what's broken, to soothe what hurts, to take away whatever trials they are facing. Sometimes we can work it out, but sometimes we can't. Sometimes we just need to wait along with them and pray that whatever challenges they face will be met and lead eventually to better times. This kind of waiting is difficult. It requires trust in God's deep love for our children—love greater even than our own. It also requires trust in the power of God to work for good in every situation. That's the kind of trust Paul was talking about in Romans. When we have that kind of trust in God, it takes the pressure off us to "fix" whatever the problem is. Even more, however, when we have that kind of trust in

God, we are better able to enter into the experiences of our children and offer not just support, but also confident hope for the future.

A Field of Dreams   *September 2000*

We had our yard reseeded last week. Actually, it was quite a project, as little had been done to the lawn in probably thirty years. As I watched the rototiller at work, I began reflecting on all that had happened in that space since we moved into our house eight years ago. We arrived in town just as it was time to start school. Each day as the boys went off, we wondered what it would be like for them as the new kids in a small town. Would they be able to break into friendships that had been going on for years? Would they find the right friends? Would they be the objects of ridicule for not knowing the way things were done in this community?

Each day they went off—Chris to seventh grade, Ben to fourth—and we'd wonder. Each day they'd come home, and we'd ask, "How was school today?" and they'd respond, "Okay." Nothing bad, but nothing great either.

Then one day it happened.

It was time for Chris to be getting home from school. Judy was at work upstairs, waiting for him. As the time passed and she began to wonder where he was, she became aware of noise coming from the backyard. Looking out the window, she discovered a wiffle-ball game in full progress. Chris and about six other boys were there, playing away.

Our house has one of the larger back yards in town. It's not huge, by any means, but bigger than most. Because it hadn't been attended to in years, it was, for the most part, a rather ugly combination of weeds and dirt. But it made a great wiffle-ball field. Chris's new friends evidently knew that, and so our yard became their official field for the next several years. Those new friends who showed up with him that day stayed friends throughout high school. In fact, at his graduation party they played one last game together for old times' sake—to celebrate their friendship and to share once again the special sense of being together that this field made possible.

Sometimes, in the middle of new and unfamiliar situations, it's hard not to worry. When the stakes are high, when people you love are involved, it's hard not to think about all that could go wrong. That's the position we found ourselves in when we moved to a new town. So many things we had no control over, so many adjustments to make, so many ways to go astray with so few established patterns to guide us.

There's probably no way to avoid the worry altogether. But in the midst of the worry it's good to have some words of reassurance. Knowing that God is there, that God is working for good and seeking the best for us and for those we love, can make all the difference. It has happened for us time and time again in life, just like it did on this field of dreams.

Questions for Reflection
1. *When have you and your family faced times of uncertainty that caused you to want to "make things right"?*

2. *Describe your response. Did it demonstrate a trust in God's ability to work things out?*

3. *What makes it difficult to have the kind of trust in God that enables you to let go of the need to "fix things" for your children?*

4. *Where in your life together as a family right now do you need to have greater confidence in God's presence seeking the best for all of you?*

5. *How can you begin to live more fully out of that confidence?*

REMEMBER RESURRECTION

Blessed be the God and Father of our Lord Jesus
Christ! By his great mercy he has given us a new birth
into a living hope through the resurrection of Jesus
Christ from the dead. (1 Peter 1:3)

What is the reason for hope? What is it that allows us, even in the midst of the trials and tribulations of being a parent, to hold on to a belief that things will work out? Our reason for hope as parents has its source, I believe, in the same source of Christian hope—the resurrection. If we have faith in the Easter miracle, then we have reason to believe in the possibility of all miracles. If we believe that God could redeem the horror of the crucifixion, then we have reason to believe that God can redeem any experience. This is our reason for hope. The ebb and flow of family life sees good times and bad. That's to be expected. The power of the resurrection is that it provides us a reason for hope in all times. And if we have hope, then it is possible to believe in what tomorrow will bring. It is possible to find strength for today and its trials. It is possible to live in the conviction that God will find a way to make things better for us. It is possible to believe—and this is the truly amazing part—that the very thing that is the source of present affliction will become the basis for a new and wondrous future.

Happy Ending   *April 2000*

The trip to New England was not what we had planned. After a continuing series of car problems, we finally got stranded in New London, Connecticut, had to leave the van and rent a car, and ended up paying more than $1,700 in repair bills. I wondered at the time whether we were cursed with everything that went wrong, or blessed because even with all the breakdowns we were never stranded and everything finally did work out.

Now, there's more to the story. Several weeks ago we got a letter from the Ford Motor Company explaining that there had been enough difficulties of the kind we had experienced that they were extending the warranty on our Windstar. If we had already had the problem fixed, they would reimburse us. And for a short period of time they would offer special incentives if we wanted to trade our older model Windstar in for a new one. Intrigued by the possibility, but doubting its feasibility, Judy and I trudged off to the Ford dealership, picked out a Windstar in the lot we liked but that cost a whole lot more money than we could afford, and headed into the show room to talk. In what seems now like a matter of seconds, we were the proud owners of a brand new 2000 Windstar. With the various special deals, special incentives, and special financing alternatives available, it turned out that we could actually afford it. After all we had gone through, a genuinely happy ending!

Wary about trivializing a major theological concept, I can't help but note that this is a pretty good picture of the way the Bible tells us God works in people's lives. Scripture sends a pretty consistent message that God can take what seems the worst of times and make them, if not the best of times, at least good times. Maybe not good in the way we would have envisioned it at first, but good nonetheless—sometimes maybe even better than we could have imagined. On that fateful trip to New England, we went, it seemed, through hell. We wildly overspent our auto repair budget. We were stressed, traumatized, and insecure. And yet, this very thing became the basis of surprising, totally unexpected good fortune.

When you get right down to it, that's really the meaning of resurrection. I know that Easter is often seen as being about bunnies or going to heaven when you die, depending on one's orientation. But it's really about God's power to redeem the worst that life can throw at us. Crucifixion becomes resurrection. Death becomes new life. Despair becomes hope.

I know from my own experience that it does not always seem that way. I know it can sound naive, maybe even shallow. I know it doesn't explain the reason for the kind of profound suffering that takes place in the world. But I also know that this is what God wants for us, that this is what God is working for in our lives. Being able to live in that kind of hope, even when there seems to be no reason for it, is what Easter is really all about.

Questions for Reflection

1. *Have you ever been surprised that a seemingly hopeless situation produced a happy ending? What happened?*

2. *Would it have been possible to experience the joy if you hadn't also experienced the pain? How are the two connected?*

3. *If this is at least part of the meaning of Easter, in what ways do you see God working to provide these kinds of "resurrection" experiences in your life and in your family?*

4. *How can you work with God to help your family experience resurrection in your life together?*

SECTION FOUR

E VEN WITH CLARITY ABOUT OUR HOPES AS PARENTS, THERE ARE *times when we just need to leave things in God's hands because we have no other reasonable alternative. At other times, however, if we cannot control what happens, we can at least control how we respond to what happens. Some of the biggest challenges we have as parents can be met more effectively if we see God at work in them and rely on God's presence and power to get us through them. Here are some of the challenges I've faced along the way:*

- ✦ **Seeing Life as a Gift**
- ✦ **Continuing to Claim and Use Gifts**
- ✦ **Being Honest**
- ✦ **Letting Hopeful Things Shape Living**
- ✦ **Remembering What It's Really All About**

SEEING LIFE AS A GIFT
"I came that they may have life, and have it abundantly." (John 10:10)

The feeling of growing old can happen no matter what age we are. Along with that feeling comes the sense that we are losing something, that something vital is slipping away from us. It may be our health, an opportunity, or perhaps even our children. It can happen when the first child goes off to kindergarten, or the last child goes off to college or work. Each year of our children's growth means saying good-bye to who they were and the way we related to them. Seen this way, growing old is a depressing prospect. But there is another way to look at it. When we understand the reality of the abundant life that Jesus talks about, growing older becomes not something to regret, but the opportunity to experience greater abundance. This is a great gift that God gives to us—if we are willing to embrace it!

Another Year   *October 2000*

I just had my fifty-fourth birthday. I've always found that "-fourth" birthdays lead to a bit more reflection than others. When you reach one of those birthdays, you can no longer say that you are in your early whatevers. So now I am no longer in my early fifties. Somehow it seems just a bit more ominous to talk about myself being in my mid-fifties.

While certain aspects of this are a bit disconcerting, it does have its positive side. John Denver wrote a song with a line that said, "It turns me on to think of growing old." I first heard it when I was in my mid-twenties. Back then it made absolutely no sense to me at all. Now, however, I know what he was talking about. Certainly, growing old has its downside. In just the past few months I've had to deal with discs and teeth that are wearing out. But it also has its upside.

In growing old, we have the opportunity to accumulate an array of rich life experiences, to deepen relationships with people who mean much to us, to see the fruits of our labors at work and in our family. So on this fifty-fourth birthday I reflected a bit. Ben provided me with a gift that demonstrated his growing maturity, as it reflected a sensitive insight into who I am and what is important to me at this point in my life. I didn't hear from Chris on my birthday. But even that was cause for celebration. He was off someplace in the remote reaches of western China far away from any means of communication, experiencing a country, a people, a way of living that is about as far away from our little town as you can get. But the very fact that he is doing that shows maturity, a wondrous interest in the world and people that is a great gift to me. And on this fifty-fourth birthday Judy and I are aware that we are about to enter a new phase in our relationship. Ben will be off to college next fall, and we will be alone again after twenty-one years with children in the house. We feel some sadness in that, of course. But also we feel excitement about the things we'll be able to do, the places we'll be able to go—just the way that things will be different for us. All of this is reason to be "turned on," as John Denver would say.

Growing old can be something that turns us on when we think of life as a gift. Then, the older we are, the bigger the gift is; the richer, deeper, fuller it becomes. So as much as I thank Judy, Chris, Ben, my family, and my friends for providing the gifts of life to me, I also thank God for the gift that is life.

Questions for Reflection
1. *In what ways have you experienced "growing old" lately?*

2. *What changes has this "aging" enabled you to see in yourself, in your children, in your relationships with others?*

3. *What are the challenges for you in growing old? What will you miss? What will be difficult to give up?*

4. *In what ways can you affirm, "It turns me on to think of growing old"?*

CONTINUING TO CLAIM AND USE YOUR GIFTS
Like good stewards of the manifold grace of God, serve one another with whatever gift each of you has received. (1 Peter 4:10)

Becoming good at anything involves consistently working to improve skills. That's no less true for parenting than it is for being a piano virtuoso or a baseball all-star. From a faith perspective, it's more than skills that we need to work on, however. One of the most basic biblical concepts is that God has "gifted" us—provided each one of us with attributes that make us who we are. The more fully we develop these gifts, the more fully we become the people God intended us to be. While some of the gifts do not apply directly to our role as parents, others, such as love, profoundly impact our relationships with our children. Becoming good as a parent involves improving the skills we learn in parenting classes, but it also involves the ongoing process of working to claim, develop, and use the gifts that God has given us. Sometimes we may be surprised by what we find. If we are open to God's work in our lives, willing at times even to be surprised by it, we will discover more gifts than we knew we had, and in the process be better parents for it.

Apple Pie Wonder   *November 1994*

I struck a blow for the liberation of all humankind last week. I baked an apple pie!

It all started on a visit to a member of the church. She was telling me how much she appreciated her daughter's visits. Among the many reasons for her appreciation was that her daughter baked the most wonderful apple pies. Well, those words were barely out of her mouth before my own personal Pavlovian reflex kicked in. I developed a deep, almost painful craving for an apple pie. After assuring her that I'd be by to visit again when her daughter was in town, I hurried off to see what could be done to satisfy the hunger at work within me.

Mrs. Smith obviously wouldn't do. Despite her claims, store-bought, frozen pies do not, cannot, and will not ever satisfy those who cherish real apple pie. Mrs. Jones wouldn't do either. Not that Judy can't make a great apple pie. But she is well beyond being busy now with all the demands of motherhood, wifehood, and self-employment. And besides, her real specialty is pumpkin. The other Mrs. Jones wouldn't do either. My mother is off enjoying herself in sunny Florida. And while she makes great apple pie (after all, that's where the craving began), even UPS Next-Day Air or USPS Priority Mail can't get the pie here in fresh-from-the-oven condition.

After I had spent a good bit of time trying to figure out what others might do for me—contemplating how they all for one reason or another had failed me; reflecting upon how I was the victim of a failed educational system that taught my sister, but not me, how to bake a pie; wondering whom I might sue for the grievous injustice that had been perpetrated on me; growing angry over how my most basic right as an American to enjoy homemade apple pie had been denied me— a strange and wondrous thing happened. I decided to bake the pie myself!

I had never baked a pie of any kind. In fact, I suffer from a pretty severe case of "crustaphobia," worrying about all the horrible things a pastry crust can do when you're mixing it, trying to roll it, and putting it in the pie pan. But overcoming even this fear, I forged ahead. I rolled it. I patted it. I marked it with a capital D (my middle initial, because everyone's a J in my family), and I put it in the oven just for me. And it was wonderful! So wonderful, in fact, that I even shared it with others so that they would know what a great pie maker I am.

I learned something important in all of this. I don't always need to look to others, either for them to do things for me or for me to blame them if they can't or don't. I have resources of my own on which to draw. Even though I am an old dog, I can still learn some new tricks. When I'm hungry, when the craving for pie or anything else sets in, I, myself, can do something about it. As God is my witness, I'll never go hungry again!

But there's more. The most important learning is that, even at my age, there's more to me than I know—more talents, more abilities, more gifts. I'm not just talking about being able to make apple pie. Sure, that proved to be an important gift. But even more important are the gifts of the Spirit that are present in me, ready to be claimed and used—not just for myself, but for others. These gifts, like the apple pie, are better by far when shared.

Questions for Reflection
1. *When have you been surprised by your ability to do something you didn't think you could do?*

2. *What are the gifts you believe God has given you? What gift have you most recently discovered?*

3. *What impact do these gifts have on your role as a parent?*

Related Activity

Sometimes our best gifts are so much a part of who we are that we need others to point them out to us. Have a conversation with a good friend about the gifts that he or she believes you have. If you learn about gifts you didn't know you had, talk about how they impact your role as a parent and ways in which you can develop them further.

BEING HONEST

O LORD, you have searched me and known me.
You know when I sit down and when I rise up;
you discern my thoughts from far away.
You search out my path and my lying down,
and are acquainted with all my ways.
Even before a word is on my tongue,
O LORD, you know it completely.
—Psalm 139:1-4

How does the realization that someone knows you that well strike you? Are you frightened by it? Do you find freedom in it? For me, it's a bit scary. But I also remember that another basic affirmation of faith is that I am loved. And then I catch a glimpse of just how wondrous God is. God knows everything there is to know about me and still loves me. It is utterly amazing. God knows everything—absolutely everything. No matter how well I've hidden it from others, God already knows. So, I must ask myself, "If I know that, why do I keep up the pretense? Who am I trying to fool?" I don't know the answer, but I do know that being honest about who I am is a key to becoming a better me. And being a better me is a key to becoming a better father.

Truth in Packaging   *June 2000*

My family had a good, long laugh the other night. We were trying out a flavor in a new line of ice cream—this one called "Strawberry Shortcake"—when Chris noticed that the cover on the container proclaimed it to be a "New Space Saver Carton." Great, we thought, until Chris read further and shared the news that this carton contained 1.75 quarts of ice cream instead of the usual half gallon!

When the laughter died down, we pondered the idiocy of the carton's claim. How many people got duped, we wondered. Did anyone really believe that the manufacturer had figured out a way to get the same amount of ice cream into a smaller carton? Then we began to wonder what other claims could have been emblazoned across the cover. Our favorite was "Same Price, Even Less Ice Cream!"

The funny part of it is that the manufacturer's claim wasn't false. The carton did take up less space. It wasn't a lie; it just didn't state the real truth. Our slogan came a lot closer to the truth than theirs. But it wouldn't have sold very much ice cream.

I was still smiling about this a day or two later when it occurred to me that in many ways, I, and probably a lot of us, aren't all that different from this ice cream carton. We're both like politicians who have learned to put the right "spin" on things. It's not that we lie, really. Rather, in an effort to present ourselves better, we choose to emphasize a fact that is really not the deeper or most important truth. The reason I overreact to a difference of opinion with one of my sons is that I'm looking out for his best interest, not that I'm opinionated and want my own way. The reason I don't help with dinner is that I have to pay some bills, not that I'm lazy and know that Judy will cook if I don't. I'm all too willing to stick the "New, Even Harder Working Husband" sticker on my forehead, when what it really should say is "Basically the Same Old Jeff."

The great problem with all of this, the great pitfall for all spin doctors, is that we begin to believe our own stuff. The more we believe it, the less honest we are with ourselves about who we really are.

This kind of honesty is, even under the best circumstances, difficult. To admit those less than positive traits, to confess that we're not the people we've made ourselves out to be, can threaten our entire self-understanding and identity. It takes great courage and fortitude. It takes willingness to be vulnerable. It also takes, I think, the knowledge that despite it all, we are still loved. In my experience, love is the only thing that gives me the courage to be deeply honest with myself about myself.

A family is a great place to experience this. Where there's real love, there also has to be real forgiveness and acceptance. If it weren't for a strong sense of my family's love for me, I wouldn't be even close to the person I am. They have enabled in me an honesty that encourages me to change and grow. The great wonder of this is that in the process of receiving this gift *from* them I become a better husband and father *for* them. As I experience this love from them, I am reminded how important it is that I share this love with them. For that is how they find the freedom to be honest with themselves, to set aside the pretense, and begin to live more fully as the people God created them to be.

Questions for Reflection

1. *Have you ever found yourself trying to put a more positive "spin" on yourself and something you have done? What would that label have read?*

2. *If there were a label on your forehead that proclaimed a real truth about yourself, what would it be?*

3. *What might the labels of other members of your family be?*

4. *What can you do to promote this kind of constructive honesty in your family?*

5. *How can that honesty be accompanied by love?*

LETTING HOPEFUL THINGS SHAPE LIVING

Whatever is true, whatever is honorable, whatever is just, whatever is pure, whatever is pleasing, whatever is commendable, if there is any excellence and if there is anything worthy of praise, think about these things. (Philippians 4:8)

It's difficult not to focus on the less positive things in life. The evening news reports what is wrong with the world. The weather channel spends most of its time talking about storms. Even idle conversations often end up being a collection of tales of woe. Over against this reality stands the counsel of Paul to focus on things that are excellent and worthy of praise. I don't believe that he's asking us to deny the reality of the troubles we encounter in our lives. Rather, he realizes that the things we focus our attention on are the things that shape our lives. Everyone experiences good and bad, joy and struggle. There's no way to avoid it. What we do have control over, however, is how we will respond to these experiences and what power we continue to let them have over us. It's true for our lives. It's true for our families as well.

Daffodils or Peeling Paint?   *April 1993*

This is the first spring in our new home. After a winter of life lived inside, we're beginning to spend a little more time in the yard. As expected, the twigs and branches left from winter storms and the last few leaves that never did get raked up in the fall mean that a good bit of work has to be done.

But some surprises also appear. There are daffodils and peeling paint. In unexpected places, totally without warning or premonition, daffodils have appeared—and crocuses and tulips. What a joy it is to be surprised by beauty! And to know that through the efforts of some previous owner, what comes as unforeseen delight this year will, in all our remaining years in this house, give the added pleasure of being keenly anticipated harbingers of spring. Such a discovery confirms our wisdom in buying this house.

But then there's the peeling paint. We've discovered that this spring as well. One feature that has always been on my list of essentials for any house we buy is a "maintenance-free exterior." I am not a house painter. Mainly, it's my fear of heights, I think. The thought of climbing that far off the ground, bucket and brush in hand, is not something I relish. Unfortunately, with each house we've purchased, the maintenance-free exterior, along with the fireplace, has always succumbed to the harsh realities of what is available and what we can afford. Someday maybe, but not this house. At any rate, the increased time we've spent outdoors has revealed a good number of places in which this newly painted house needs further work. I am not happy about it.

Beyond the delight of daffodils and the pain of peeling paint, however, these discoveries have left me with a fundamental choice. Which of these is going to shape my attitude about the house in which we live? Both are part of the reality of this house. Both are things I will need to deal with as long as I remain the owner of this house. But which one will determine the way I feel about this house? Will it be the daffodils or the peeling paint? I haven't begun to paint yet, so I remain full of hope. I hope the daffodils win out. Life in this house will certainly be more pleasant for my family and me if they do. For it will be a life of delight with some necessary pain to deal with, rather than a life of pain with a few fleeting moments of delight.

That's the kind of choice that faces most of us pretty regularly in our family life. There's the peeling paint of dashed dreams and bruised relationships, of broken promises and failed potential, perhaps even children not living up to our expectations for them. But there are also the daffodils of love and beauty, of finding common cause with others who care for the same things we do, of making our life and family what we know they can be. It can be a life of delight with some necessary pain to deal with or a life of pain with fleeting moments of delight. And we do have a choice about what reality will shape the rest of our life. Will it be the peeling paint or the surprising daffodils?

Questions for Reflection

1. *When have you been faced with similar life situations of mixed blessings?*

2. *What are the "daffodils" and the "peeling paint" of your life right now?*

3. *What will help you focus on the "daffodils" of your life?*

REMEMBERING WHAT IT'S REALLY ALL ABOUT

*And Noah with his sons and his wife and his sons'
wives went into the ark to escape the waters of the
flood. (Genesis 7:7)*

My guess is that Noah had one of the most intense experiences
of family life in the history of humankind. Imagine being
cooped up in that small space with your entire family and all
those animals for such a long time. There must have been mess-
es of every kind to clean up. When you think about it that way,
Noah's drunken behavior immediately following this ordeal
becomes a bit more understandable! But Noah and his family
made it, and because they did, we humans were given another chance. Although the Bible doesn't tell us about it, we may
ponder with interest what was at work in their life together
that made it all possible.

Getting Wet   *October 1998*

I just spent three of the wettest days of my life.

I was in Maine for parents' weekend at Chris's college. It rained. And it rained. And it rained some more. We endured a veritable deluge the entire weekend. This was supposed to be a time of walking leisurely around the campus, of going to the football game, of enjoying the splendors of the fall foliage. Instead, it was a time of getting wet.

When we were supposed to be enjoying the pleasures of a reception on the college president's lawn, we, along with just about everyone else in the entire state of Maine, were in the L. L. Bean store trying to dry out. Virtually none of the specific plans we had for the weekend worked out the way we thought they would.

Life is like that. At least, every now and then it is. No matter how much we plan, no matter how high our hopes, it just doesn't work out the way it's supposed to. Sometimes it's better, more often it's not.

Something else about the weekend was a lot like life. We got through it. And we actually enjoyed ourselves. Without pushing it too much, I came up with three things that helped that happen. First, we had each other—people who know and care about each other were sharing this experience. Noah had his family in the ark. I had mine in the Windstar. Somehow that made the whole thing much more bearable.

Second, we had the ability to laugh. I don't know what Noah and his family did to pass the time, but I can't help but believe that they found some measure of fun even in the midst of their predicament. That's what happened to us. You can only get so wet before the utter ridiculousness of trying to keep dry becomes laughable. So laugh we did. Through the wind and rain. Through the puddles. Through the drizzle and the downpour. We laughed.

Third, and most important, we kept remembering what the weekend was really all about. I imagine that that was important for Noah too. The creature comforts of the ark couldn't have been all that great. Remembering why they were there and what God had in mind for them certainly would have helped Noah and his family to cope. That's the way it worked for us. It wasn't about foliage and receptions or keeping dry and looking nice. It was about being together again as a family after the six weeks that Chris had been away from home. No amount of rain changed that. It would have been plain foolish of us to let mere water interfere with what we were really about.

I know that the kinds of problems we encounter in life are a lot more significant than several inches of rain. And yet I can't help but think that the three things that helped us that weekend would also help get all of us through most of the things life throws at us.

Into each life a little rain must fall, the saying goes. When it happened to Noah, he had his family to keep him going. I had the same good fortune. When it happens to you, may you remain surrounded by those who know you and care about you, may you retain the ability to laugh, and may you regain your focus on what is most important in this life.

It might just keep you going until the sun comes out again.

Questions for Reflection
1. *What experiences have you shared as a family in which the reality was far different from what you had planned and anticipated?*

2. *What was it that kept you going during those experiences?*

3. *Where do you see these three things at work in your own family life?*
- affirming that you have each other no matter what happens
- maintaining the ability to laugh
- remembering what it is really all about

SECTION FIVE

T*HE CHALLENGES WE FACE AS PARENTS CONTINUE TO BE THE topic of discussion in this section:*

- ✦ Taking a Stand
- ✦ Giving Thanks When the Going Gets Tough
- ✦ Letting Children Teach
- ✦ Speaking Truth with Love and Laughter
- ✦ Relying on God's Forgiving Love

TAKING A STAND

Do not be conformed to this world, but be transformed by the renewing of your minds, so that you may discern what is the will of God—what is good and acceptable and perfect. (Romans 12:2)

Has anyone really solved the problem yet? How do we bring our children up in the world without them being conformed to it? How do we help them deal with the barrage of worldly things and still retain values that are compatible with the gospel? That's always been difficult, but it's even harder now. The cyclonic pace of change in the world means that we have even less solid ground on which to stand. We as adults can barely figure out what's going on. How can we expect our children to get it? Or, perhaps even more threatening, our children understand the world better than we do, and we have even less basis for sorting out what's compatible with the gospel than they do! It's the same everywhere you turn—from sex to consumerism, from win-at-all-cost competition to drugs-and-alcohol escapism. It is a long, complex, and tricky maze we're caught in. We know where it can lead if we get through it the right way—to those things that are good, acceptable, and perfect. But every wrong turn has its consequences, every hesitation its cost. Sometimes we just need to stop and declare what we believe, whether anyone is listening or not. It will be good for us. And it just may provide something for our children to hang on to as well.

The Real Holiday Priority   *November 2000*

Once again I begin the Christmas season vowing not to be done in by the commercialism that abounds at this time of year. I promise to become neither a victim of it nor so reactive to it that I can't enter into the genuine spirit of buying so that I can give to others. Over the years I have found this an all but impossible task. And I've found it even more difficult to engage my entire family in this perspective. The world demands so much of us at Christmas time that it's hard to focus on Christ.

This year is no exception. I was doing pretty well, actually. I was maintaining that painstakingly delicate balance between spirituality and consumerism—not an easy undertaking by any means. But I had reason to believe that after years of practice I was going to be able to stay the course—at least until the first of December.

Then it happened. I got interested in a football game and was deluged by a flood of automobile commercials. They were all for the same company, but a number of different models. The ads were extolling the low interest rate available on loans. Each and every one of them concluded with these words: "Savings that let you spend more on a real holiday priority—yourself." That did it!

What holiday has that priority, I wondered. The holidays I'm familiar with at this time of year all emphasize the importance of giving to others, not getting for yourself. Christmas actually celebrates the birth of someone who said, "It is more blessed to give than to receive," and that if we really want to find ourselves we need to lose ourselves, not spend more money on ourselves.

I suppose I could chalk it all up to a woeful ignorance of the religious tradition that is the basis for this holiday season. But then I remembered. The people who do these commercials are not ignorant people. They may not know much about religious traditions, but they do know about people and what motivates them. That is, after all, what they get paid for.

So, what's really troubling about these commercials is the fact that there must be a good body of evidence that says that the way to motivate people is to appeal to their selfishness.

Knowing full well that I will not reach anywhere near the number of people who heard those commercials, I still feel compelled to challenge their assumptions and assertion. It is a gross distortion of these holidays to say that their priority is doing something for yourself. It is a gross misrepresentation of truth to claim that fulfillment in life comes from making yourself a priority. It's not about self; it's about others. It's not about getting; it's about giving. It's not about buying; it's about loving. That is the real, and only true, holiday priority.

Questions for Reflection

1. *What has your experience been as you have tried to focus on preparation for the birth of Christ in the midst of the commercialism of the Christmas season? What ways have you and your family developed to cope with it?*

2. *What are other concerns for which you believe you need to help your children develop a perspective that is different from the world's?*

3. *What struggles have you had in doing that?*

4. *In what ways does your faith strengthen your ability to do it?*

GIVING THANKS WHEN THE GOING GETS TOUGH

Rejoice always, pray without ceasing, give thanks in all circumstances; for this is the will of God in Christ Jesus for you. (1 Thessalonians 5:16-18)

Every family has those experiences that test their mettle. Sometimes they find themselves in the midst of tragedy. Sometimes it just seems as though circumstances conspire to make life extremely trying. In the midst of these times it's pretty difficult to find reasons to be joyful. And yet, there it is, right there in Paul's first letter to the Thessalonians: the exhortation to rejoice always. How are we to do such a thing? Or perhaps, even more basically, how are we to avoid thinking that this is just plain impossible advice? I admit that I struggle with it. But I also have to confess that I take the Bible very seriously, so if it's in the Book, I want to figure out how I can apply it to my life. The key, I think, comes with the preposition. Paul said we are to give thanks in all circumstances, not for all circumstances.

There's a big difference. "For all circumstances" would be impossible, if not just plain stupid. "In all circumstances" opens the door of possibility. It asks us not to be thankful for everything that happens to us, but even in the midst of things that we are decidedly not thankful for to find reason to give thanks. It encourages us to look deeply and to see differently. It asks us to see God at work and to give thanks for that and rejoice.

Curse or Blessing? February 2000

My family and I have been through some tough times together these past several weeks, so the thought of time away had great appeal for all of us. The plan was simple enough. Judy, Ben, and I would drive to Maine to pick up Chris at college and bring him home for winter break. We'd take an extra day for Chris and Ben to ski and for Judy and me to have some time for ourselves. We'd even throw in a tour of the campus of one of the colleges Ben is interested in. It had all the makings of a great family weekend, but, as the saying goes, "The best laid plans. . . ."

We planned to leave on Friday, but sleet and freezing rain postponed our departure a day. We planned to leave on Saturday, but car trouble fifteen miles into the trip forced us to turn around, have a full tune up, and wait yet another day. On Sunday we left town and made it uneventfully to Maine. When we arrived, however, the temperature gauge started moving up and up. We stopped at a gas station, added some antifreeze, and prayed. But the problem persisted, so we stopped at an auto repair shop, had the mechanic look it over, and prayed. He made a few adjustments and the gauge was back to normal again. Off we went to L. L. Bean and the Freeport outlet stores. All was well again— or so we thought.

Monday was the day to ski. The snow was great. The boys enjoyed themselves immensely. Judy and I did our errands, kept constant watch over the temperature gauge, and prayed. We picked up the boys and headed south again, planning to reach Connecticut that night. By the time we hit Rhode Island, however, the temperature gauge was reaching new heights. We coasted into a gas station off the highway. It had to have been the only station in the entire state that had a mechanic on duty at ten o'clock on a holiday night. He explained why what we had done before didn't solve the problem, made some new adjustments, and set us on our way with the temperature gauge right where it should be. We prayed some more, reached Connecticut by midnight, and had a good night's sleep. Tuesday morning we drove to the campus, thinking all was well at last. We should have known better.

Two minutes after the campus tour was over, we were coasting off the highway as the temperature gauge skyrocketed yet again. This time we not only prayed, but also used our newly acquired cell phone to call the only Ford dealer listed in the phone book. It turned out that we were just a mile away. Setting forth cautiously and praying all the way, we made it there. I explained what we'd been through. The service manager gave me the great news that I had described the "classic symptoms" of a problem they could fix in about four days for $1,200. Although I was sorely tempted to head to the showroom and plunk down twenty-five thousand dollars to a buy a new minivan, reality and the laughter of my family took hold. It was evidently apparent to them that it would be rather difficult to do that with a checking account balance that averages about $34.17. So off we went to the car rental office to rent the biggest car they had—the only one that had the remote possibility of holding all of our accumulated luggage and purchases, plus Chris's skis. We finally made it home on Tuesday evening, only two hours later than the master plan had anticipated.

So, how are we to understand what happened on that fateful weekend? Was it, as Chris commented at one point, "a debacle," a series of weather and car trouble curses? Or, was it a series of blessings? We always found someone who could get us together for the next phase of the journey; we were never stranded; this was the first time we ever had a cell phone with us; when it was finally apparent that the old Windstar would get us no further, the Ford dealer was right down the road; the car rental office was right next door; my credit card has a higher limit than my checking account balance; we encountered a whole array of people who gladly and caringly did what they could to help us out; we all made it home together and safely.

I'm not at all eager to go through a weekend precisely like this one again, and am certainly not thankful for everything that happened to us. I do, however, see all the blessings that the weekend contained. Even in the midst of the trauma they provided reason to give thanks. Paul, I guess, had it right. It is possible to give thanks, not necessarily *for* all things, but certainly *in* all things!

Questions for Reflection

1. *When have you found blessings for you and your family in the midst of difficult times? Who were the people who provided the blessings for you? What did they do?*

2. *Describe a time in which you made a conscious choice to focus on the blessings in a difficult situation and give thanks for them?*

3. *How does an attitude of thanksgiving affect your ability to cope with such a situation? How does prayer?*

LETTING CHILDREN TEACH

Your sons and daughters shall prophesy, . . . and your young men shall see visions. (Joel 2:28)

The usual pattern is that parents are the ones who teach and children are the ones who learn. There are, of course, exceptions to that. Children, for example, are most decidedly the ones who teach parents patience and perseverance. But when it comes to content or skills, we usually think of parents as the ones who do the teaching. After all, we know more. Every now and then, however, we come across something that reminds us that this assumption has its exceptions. Children can teach us much about life, how to look at it, and how to cope with it. They can remind us of what we have lost sight of in the pursuit of whatever it is we adults pursue. They can even, without knowing it, teach us about our relationship with God. In order for any of this to happen, however, we need to be open to it. We need to put ourselves in the position of the learner, go humbly to our children, and let them teach. Wondrous things can happen when we do. We will hear great prophecies and see great visions. And our lives and faith will be deeper and richer because we did.

Stacking   *September 2001*

The other night I walked in on Ben while he was studying—at least, that's what he said he was doing. This is what I saw: a book was open on his desk with a pad next to it on which he was taking notes; his computer was on at one of his favorite web sites about cars; he was engaged in at least three conversations with friends using the "instant messenger" feature of the computer; the stereo was playing a new CD; a rerun of *Seinfeld* was on the TV. This is studying? Every fiber of my being wanted to cry out, "Turn off the stereo, turn off the TV, turn off the computer, and start concentrating on the book! That's what studying is!" I didn't do that, however. It took a great effort, but I held my tongue. I did ask him what he was studying. (At least he knew.) And I did comment that I'd find it hard to study with all that other stuff going on. (He took it pretty well.) But I didn't berate him and I didn't order him to do anything.

Part of the reason for that is that I've been doing some reading about the postmodern age we're supposedly entering and the skills that are needed to function in such an age. One of them is multitasking, or stacking. That is what Ben was doing. It's a learned skill, the experts in such things say—one that we modern-age people didn't develop, but younger people are. I think that's true, although I do have respect for women who tell me that multitasking is what being a mother is all about. At any rate, I figured that if this was a skill Ben needed to develop in order to survive and thrive in the new age we're entering, I'd better let him have a go at it. The real test will be to wait and see what happens to his grades.

As often happens, I kept thinking about this experience. And the more I thought about it, the more I realized that I could learn a thing or two from Ben. Stacking is the ability to handle a number of sensory experiences at the same time, to integrate them in some fashion, and then to develop meaning from that integration. It's a whole lot different from the way I learned, which probably had more to do with fitting things into boxes of understanding than it did with finding meaning in how things fit together. As I have been doing my thinking, I've been wondering if this is a skill that might actually benefit my relationship with God. After all, what use is there in trying to fit God into a box so we can understand God better? That's about as fool-hardy a pursuit as you can come up with. Wouldn't it be better to be able to experience God along with the other things that impact my life and then find meaning in the way they come together?

I think that Ben and the postmoderns may well be on to something. I hope I can keep learning from them.

Questions for Reflection
1. *What are some of the things you have learned from your children?*

2. *How have you and how might you develop the ability to be quiet long enough to learn from them?*

3. *How do you approach your relationship with God? Is it to put God in a box in order to understand, or is to find meaning in the way in which God fits together with the other aspects of your life?*

SPEAKING TRUTH WITH LOVE AND LAUGHTER
"You will know the truth and the truth will make you free." (John 8:32)

Families are great places for making known the truth. Certainly, a lot has been said about "family secrets" or the things everyone knows you simply do not talk about. That is part of the picture in many families. There is another possibility, however. The deeper truths about ourselves are all but impossible to hide in the family. Being together that much time, relating to each other that intimately, reveals much about who we are and what makes us tick. Other family members see the truth about us— even those truths we'd rather not face. That could be a threatening and potentially damaging reality. But in a family, there is also love that tempers truth. That love provides gentleness to the speaking of truth. It also lets us laugh with a person as truths are named. This love means we laugh with the person, not at the person. One is a sign of love, the other of ridicule. When both love and laughter live in a family, the truth can be powerfully spoken. And when it is, even though it might be painful, we will be set free.

Sometimes It Hurts   *October 1991*
Chris, Ben, and I were playing a game called "Outburst Junior" the other night. In this game, you are given a category and have to name specific items that fit within it. If the category is automobiles, for example, you have to name Ford, Nissan, Buick, and so forth.

Ben drew the category "things you have two of on your head." He named eyes and ears quickly, but got stuck at that point. Being the good and ever helpful father, I tried to prompt him. "Things you have two of on your head," I said. "Look at me." Without pausing even so much as a second, he yelled out, "Chins!"

We all laughed uproariously. I probably laughed a bit less than my sons, however. For the fact is, sometimes when you come face to face with the truth about yourself, it hurts. I'm well aware that I have at least two chins. I'm reminded of that every morning when I shave.

And I'm well aware that others know this about me as well. You can't look at me and not know it. And yet, even though I know it and I know that everyone else knows it, when this reality is stated aloud, it hurts. Maybe it's embarrassment, maybe it's vanity, or maybe it's the blunt reminder that I'm not really the person I would like to be. Whatever the reason, sometimes the truth hurts.

This is, of course, a silly illustration of that fact. Stating the deeper truths about ourselves, who we are, how we act, and what motivates us, can be much more painful than this.

All this has led me to ponder Jesus' words about truth making you free. Had it been up to me, I don't think "free" is the word I would have chosen. The truth will make you cry, perhaps. Or the truth will cause you to reflect. Maybe even the truth will help you grow. But make you free?

So, how does it work? I think that it comes down to this. Truth sets us free, because living a lie is a painful captivity of the spirit and the soul. The pain of facing the reality of my double chin is offset by the freedom I discover when it becomes apparent that this doesn't make any difference to Ben or to most everyone else. Avoiding the truth kept me captive to worry and wondering what people might think of me, captive to my own images of myself. Stating the truth freed me from that captivity.

The same dynamic works for more profound issues, too. If our families can be places where we can face truth, then they have the potential to be places of deep insight and profound growth. Of course, the truth must be shared with love. And a bit of laughter always helps, as well. Neither love nor humor will remove the sometimes painful realizations truth-telling brings to us, but they can soften the blow because they are signs of genuine caring and support.

Being a parent can be a painful experience for many reasons. One of them certainly is that the intimate relationships of parenthood will invariably bring us face to face with ways we fail our children even though our intentions are the best, ways we hurt our children even though that's the last thing we want to do. These things will happen. They are inevitable. When they do, our unwillingness to face the truth about them enslaves us. Facing and sharing the truth, as painful as it may be, has the potential to free us from that enslavement—maybe not immediately, but certainly over time as love and laughter continue their work upon us.

Questions for Reflection
1. *What traits of each of your family members are you able to laugh about together? Do you find freedom in this laughter?*

2. *When have you or a member of your family discovered a new sense of freedom in being able to share a truth that had been kept hidden?*

3. *What role does laughter play in your family and its ability to speak the truth?*

4. *How might you increase the level of acceptance within your family?*

RELYING ON GOD'S FORGIVING LOVE

If we confess our sins, he who is faithful and just will forgive us our sins and cleanse us from all unrighteousness. (1 John 1:9)

As good as we may be at this parenting thing, there will always be times when what we do or say just isn't what it should have been. We will be short-tempered rather than patient, self-centered rather than self-giving, judgmental rather than accepting. It will happen. It will happen more often than we care to admit. This can lead to a great sense of failure and guilt. We all know how delicate children can be, how sometimes just a word can have a powerfully negative impact on them. This is a heavy burden to bear. It might become an unbearable burden, one that debilitates us or causes us to act out in inappropriate ways that have a further negative impact on our children. Fortunately, God provides a way out. It's a simple thing called forgiveness. God is ready to forgive us for whatever we have done or said. If we experience that forgiveness, the burden is lifted and we are free to begin again. It is, I think, one of the most essential dynamics involved in being a parent.

Starting Over   *January 1993*

I do not believe in New Year's resolutions. In fact, in my more cynical moments I believe that they are really part of a monstrous and sinister plot cooked up by people who take great joy in making others feel guilty. I don't make New Year's resolutions any more, but when I did, the process went something like this.

Phase one began in December. In this time when I should have been reflecting on the joy of Christmas, I would instead be thinking about everything that was wrong with me. After all, you can't decide what to change about yourself unless you first know what's wrong with you. I'd find myself making a list and checking it twice, or maybe even five, six, or seven times: I am overweight; I am not as patient with the kids as I should be; I am not as sensitive toward my wife as she is toward me. From this list of problem areas I would then select two or three that were ripe for resolutions.

When I wrote the resolutions, they always sounded like very formal, important documents. A typical one would come out sounding something like this: Whereas, all of Jeffrey Jones's pants are too tight; whereas, his double chin is fast becoming triple; whereas, he persists in his addiction to chocolate chip cookies; now, therefore, be it resolved that the aforementioned Jeffrey Jones will commence and continue to follow an approved weight-reduction regimen until such time as he has lost ten or fifteen or twenty pounds—depending on just how bad a year it has been.

After weeks of grueling self-examination and self-recrimination, the resolution was made, and I entered phase two. Early in January I'd go back to the office, and there, at the very first coffee break, what to my wondering eyes should appear but leftover treats and temptations galore! Of course, these were brought in by folks who had made similar resolutions about weight loss and so wanted to unload all their Christmas goodies on some other poor souls.

At home I'd be rummaging around in the refrigerator looking for a carton of cottage cheese I was just dying to eat, and way at the back I would find a neatly wrapped package of chocolate-covered cherries. A little voice would say, "Just one won't hurt." A bigger voice would say, "Who cares about the diet, anyway!" Despite all my preparation, all my good intentions, I would give into temptation.

Then phase three began. It would last all of February, and often into March. It was the phase of intense guilt, knowing that I had failed again, knowing that this year's resolution had gone the way of the one I made last year, and the year before that, and the year before that.

This, I concluded, was not a process by which one could enhance one's self-esteem. So I quit making New Year's resolutions.

We have, however, another way to change, to grow, and to better ourselves. It's based in the very simple idea that God loves us. In that love, God is ready to forgive us for all the ways we have failed, ready to lead us into the kind of life God intends for us to have.

This way isn't necessarily an easy way either. It means taking stock, admitting failures, starting out in a new direction. But there are some important differences. This way emphasizes not guilt, but love—God's love—a love that always forgives. This way can happen any time of year, not just in January.

This way doesn't leave us all alone to do the hard work of changing. It gives us a companion: the one who knows what it's like and has all the strength that is needed. That's enough to make the celebration last not just one night, but all year long.

Questions for Reflection

1. *What has been your experience in making New Year's resolutions?*

2. *In what ways has God's forgiving love for you enabled you to face yourself as you are and make needed changes?*

3. *Where have you found sources of support as you make changes in your life?*

Related Activity

In your family, make commitments to each other and to God about ways in which you want to change in the coming weeks, months, or year. Share the support you will need to help make this change and plan for ways in which you can offer this support to one another.

Section Six

PARENTING IS ABOUT MEETING THE GREAT CHALLENGES OF BEING A *family. But it's also about living day to day. From a faith perspective, it's about living day to day with an awareness of the presence of God, a sense of the way God is at work in what you are about. Relational skills play an important part of that day-to-day living. Here are some of the ones that have been particularly helpful to me along the way:*

- ✦ **Know When to Lay Back**
- ✦ **Learn to Let Go While Staying Connected**
- ✦ **Expect to Be Surprised**
- ✦ **Cherish the Moment**
- ✦ **Take a Break**

KNOW WHEN TO LAY BACK
For my thoughts are not your thoughts, nor are your ways my ways, says the LORD. (Isaiah 55:8)

Over the years it's become fairly apparent to me that Isaiah was right: God's ways are not my ways. As much as I'd like it to be, it simply isn't the case. I have not yet discovered the magic formula that lets me attune myself to God in all things at all times. Nor have I found any way at all to get God to think like me! In fact, this insight applies even more broadly. My wife's ways are not my ways, nor are my sons'. Part of the challenge of being a family is figuring out how people with different ways can coexist in fairly close proximity without one or the other of them losing their identity or integrity—or mind.

Getting Out of the Way   *May 1998*

Chris has just finished the long, arduous process of applying to colleges, waiting to discover which ones accepted him, and then deciding where to go. In my house, as in the houses of high school seniors across the land, there was great rejoicing on May 1, the day when many colleges must be notified whether or not you will attend. All things considered, he probably handled the whole thing better than I did.

The dean of admissions at one of the schools to which Chris applied warned me over a year ago that it would be a difficult time. His advice was to relax, lay back as much as possible, and let Chris handle it. He predicted, quite rightly, that Chris would do it differently than I would, differently than I wanted him to do it, but he would get it done. I've spent the last year trying to heed that advice. Sometimes I did a good job; other times I failed miserably. But now that it's all over, I am convinced that the good dean was right.

What I had to learn was patience, along with a healthy dose of humility. After all, it was Chris who was going to college, not me. Sure, I knew more about the process than he did. I could probably predict more accurately what things would impress what colleges, and I could be a whole lot more organized in the way I approached it. But it was his college; it needed to be his decision and it would only lead to trouble if I tried to make it for him or even just pushed him in the direction I wanted him to go. I needed to let go and trust both him and the process.

Looking back on the whole thing, I think I did a fairly good job of that. To my amazement, the times I did it well were also the times things moved along most easily, the times Chris felt best about what was going on. In the end, the decision was his. At this point, it's hard for me to imagine a better outcome. It's amazing what can happen if we just get out of the way!

That's a lesson that I see applying to many experiences in being a parent. Growing, maturing children need to learn to make their own decisions. They'll never be able to make the big ones, unless they've had some practice making the small ones. This requires that patient humility with their own pace and process of decision making needs to be exercised even when they are quite young. Perhaps it would have been a bit easier for me if I had gotten more practice along the way.

It also occurs to me that this lesson applies to my relationship with God. More often than not I have a pretty good idea of what God should be doing in my life and in the world. I've also got a pretty good idea of how God should be doing it. Armed with this knowledge, it's quite easy to set out to cajole, encourage, entice, push, manipulate, and bargain God into doing the "right" thing.

What's really needed, however, is the patience and humility simply to get out of God's way and let God do it. What I'm after won't necessarily happen on my schedule, and most likely not in the way I would have done it. But if I can learn to lay back in my relationship with God, it could well be that the results will please me as much as they did when I did that with Chris. At the very least, it's worth a try.

Questions for Reflection

1. *When has tension occurred between you and one of your children over the nature and process of a decision that he or she was making?*

2. *In what ways might approaching these situations with patience and humility help?*

3. *How might that same type of humility enrich your relationship with God?*

LEARN TO LET GO WHILE STAYING CONNECTED

Therefore, my beloved, just as you have always obeyed me, not only in my presence, but much more now in my absence, work out your own salvation with fear and trembling; for it is God who is at work in you, enabling you both to will and to work for his good pleasure. (Philippians 2:12-13)

Letting go of our children is one of the most difficult things we do. We know from the very moment of their birth that this is the purpose of our relationship with them—to set them free. We love, teach, train, equip, rebuke, punish, forgive, and love some more, all so that at some point in their lives they can leave us. On the surface it sounds almost ludicrous, really—to devote ourselves so completely to something we won't be able to keep. And when the reality of their leaving hits home for us, the pain can be intense. It takes great effort not to stand in the way of the letting go. I think that is the issue that Paul was struggling with in his letter to the Philippian Christians. They had obeyed him in the past, much as children. But now he is encouraging them to strike out on their own, to work out their own salvation. It is a process of letting go. Paul can do this because of his confidence that God is at work in them. That confidence is also essential for us as parents as we begin the sometimes painful process of letting go. For us, as it must have been for Paul, it is a profound experience of love and loss. It is also one of the ways we gain insight into the depth of God's love for us.

Coming Home Again   *May 2000*

Chris arrives home from college today. He just finished his sophomore year. I'm eager to see him again. And yet I wonder what it will be like.

The truth of the matter is that he is really growing, not just older and more mature, but also away. All year long I've had this feeling that each time I say good-bye to him he is going just a bit further away from home and me. I've felt that way despite the fact that during the past few months he's actually talked longer with us when he calls home. But what we talk about is the life he is establishing—a life in which Judy and I are playing a different and less significant role. Those conversations reveal his increasingly independent thinking and both a desire and an ability to make his own decisions. So, in them we learn about weekend trips to Boston he's made with friends, plans to spend a week in North Carolina with his high school friends this summer, and, by the way, that he is going to China to study next semester.

This summer we will carpool together to work—two hours a day in the car. It should be interesting. I predict some long periods of silence. I hope also for times of laughter, talk about the trials and tribulations of the Red Sox, and moments when we will share deeply and significantly about our lives and ourselves. We won't dwell on those moments, to be sure. It's not our way. But I think they will be there, and I will cherish them.

This kind of independence, this moving away, is what Judy and I as parents have been striving for for Chris's entire life. Now that it is happening, we celebrate it. We also grieve, at least a bit. For something important to us is changing and will never be the same. Someone who has shaped our lives and who we are is going away, even though he is coming home for the summer. It is a time of wonderment for us.

This experience isn't unique. It's been part of the human experience ever since parents started having children. In fact, it's really a dynamic that God set in place with the creation of human beings. We were created to bring forth new life, to nurture that life, and to let it go. Parents have been doing that since the beginning of time. And still, after all these years, the letting go is a difficult thing to do.

I can't help but think that God feels the same way about us. God created us, even made us in the divine image. God invested everything in us. But it wasn't to keep us; it was to let us go. So, even as I go through this experience with Chris, God is undoubtedly thinking about me—wondering how well I'll exercise the freedom I have been given, wondering how often I'll phone home and talk about my life, wondering if everything will be okay with me—celebrating and grieving all at the same time. It's a wonderment.

Questions for Reflection

1. *How have you experienced "growing away" in your children? How have you experienced "growing away" from your parents?*

2. *How have you celebrated this change? How have you grieved it?*

3. *How have you maintained "connectedness" in the face of this change? How might you?*

4. *In what ways does God experience this same dynamic in relationship with you? How can you maintain "connectedness" in your relationship with God?*

EXPECT TO BE SURPRISED

For by grace you have been saved through faith, and this is not your own doing; it is the gift of God—not the result of works, so that no one may boast. (Ephesians 2:8-9)

It runs counter to just about everything we've learned about life. It is something we do not deserve, something that no matter how hard we try, we can never earn. And yet it is one of the greatest gifts ever given. It is the gift of salvation. And it only comes through grace. That's impossible to understand. More than one theologian has gotten lost in the attempt. Countless believers have had their faith challenged trying to do it. Even though we ask all the questions we can think of, we will never understand. Certainly, God's love for us helps, but it doesn't explain it, for love that deep and expansive is something we can never really understand either. In the final analysis, all we can do is accept it and be willing to be surprised by it. Many of life's best gifts are like that. We can't understand; we must simply accept—accept and celebrate.

Out of the Blue *August 2000*

Judy and I each were surprised by our sons this summer. Quite unexpectedly, they each did something that provided a special time to cherish.

Ben showed up after work one day with a dozen roses for his mother. She was, needless to say, shocked by this. I was full of questions: Why did he do that? How did he afford that? What had he done wrong? For Judy it was different. "It's that he did it that matters," she said. The joy of seeing this in my son was only slightly dampened by the realization that never in almost twenty-five years of marriage had Judy ever received a dozen roses from me. Put to shame by my own son! Can you believe it? At any rate, those roses graced the table in our dining room for a week, the memory of them continuing to glow, at least in Judy's heart. And, taking the hint provided by Ben, I gave Judy roses for our anniversary.

Chris surprised me in a quite different way. One afternoon he asked, "Dad, do you want to go to the Phillies and Red Sox game tonight?" In order to grasp the full meaning of this, you need to understand that although I grew up in New England, our family has never lived there. I have, however, always considered it one of my sacred duties as a father to make Red Sox fans of my sons. We've made pilgrimages to Fenway Park; we've agonized over pennant races gone awry; we've cheered the exploits of Roger Clemens and more recently of Pedro Martinez. At least in this one area of my fatherly obligations, I have been an unqualified success! So when Chris asked me to go to the game with him, it meant a lot. I didn't quite understand why. But I found myself saying, "It's that he did it that matters." So what if the Red Sox lost—to the Phillies, no less! We still had a great time.

These unexpected serendipities mean a lot in life. One or two can keep you going for a long time—*if* you learn to recognize them and cherish them. In faith circles this kind of thing is called grace. It's the unexpected, undeserved surprises that God throws at us every now and then. You can't explain it, really. You can't understand why God would do such a thing. All you can do is sit back, stop asking questions or trying to figure out why, and simply say, "It's that he did it that matters." If you can do that, accept it for what it is and continue to cherish it, a single moment of grace can get you through a whole long string of difficult days.

Questions for Reflection

1. *Can you remember when one of your children pleasantly surprised you with something he or she said or did? How did you respond: question the motivation, wonder why, simply accept and celebrate it?*

2. *When have you experienced this surprising grace in your relationship with God? How did you respond?*

3. *What difference do these moments of surprising grace make for you?*

CHERISH THE MOMENT

We always give thanks to God for all of you and mention you in our prayers, constantly remembering before our God and Father your work of faith and labor of love and steadfastness of hope in our Lord Jesus Christ. (1 Thessalonians 1:2-3)

"Cherish" is a word we use to describe the way we feel about the depth of caring and appreciation in a relationship. Paul had that kind of relationship with the people in the churches he founded and with those he ministered. When he writes about always giving thanks for the people, he is talking about cherishing them. When he writes about remembering their work of faith, he is talking about cherishing the moments he had with them. It wasn't a traditional family, but it had many of the elements of one. For that reason, Paul's relationship with churches can provide insights for us into our family relationships. In the midst of daily life and living it is sometimes difficult for us to remember and to talk about how deeply thankful we are, how vitally important these family relationships are to us. Often, only when we experience the distance of death do we know what we are missing. It would be good, in a sense, if we could live each day with the reality of death fresh in our minds—not to be morbid, but to help us see differently and appreciate more fully, to help us cherish the moment that we have and live accordingly.

Holiday Preparations   *November 2000*

We've made some good plans for the holidays this year. My sister and my mother and Judy's mother will be joining us for Thanksgiving. This means that there will be more people sitting around our table that day than there have been in a number of years. In this special time for family, it really is a matter of "the more the merrier," so I'm looking forward to a great day.

We'll be celebrating Christmas in two parts. The first will be at our house with our family and Judy's mom. Then the four of us will travel to Florida for a few days with my sister and mother. I'm sure that in the midst of all the traveling, we'll find plenty of time for singing Christmas carols and listening to the Christmas story, so that we won't forget what the season is all about.

Sandwiched between these two traditional events will be a rather unique one for us. Sometime around December 9th we'll make a trip to the international airport in Philadelphia to meet Chris as he returns from a semester of study in China. He will have been away from home for more than three months. We've kept in pretty good touch through regular e-mail and the occasional phone call, but actually seeing him again will be something special for all of us.

Our reunion with him will be great, but it will also force us to deal with something that will be a big part of this holiday season for all of us. This will be the first Thanksgiving and Christmas since my father died. We won't have any reunions with him this holiday season—none at all in this world. I know what is said about the first major holidays following the death of a loved one. I know it's not easy, because the pain of separation is that much greater in those times when memories are strong and feelings deep. I'm not quite certain what it will be like for me.

I don't want to ignore the grief that will be a part of these coming days. But I would like to experience that grief with the understanding that it is as great as it is only because of how much my father meant and continues to mean to me. A potent relationship exists between the depth of our grief for someone who has died and the depth of the love we shared with that person. Even in the pain, that is something to cherish.

My other hope is that this grief will lead me to a deeper awareness of how important all the members of my family are to me, how much they have shaped the person I am. I will grieve for them too when they are gone. But while they are here, I hope I can cherish each moment we have to the fullest. I hope I can focus on the things about them that bring richness and beauty to my life. I hope the deep love I have for them will be evident every minute of our time together, both in what I say to them and how I treat them.

I won't be alone in grieving this holiday season. Certainly, the other members of my family will do so. But also, so many others will be grieving—almost everyone, in fact. For we have all suffered loss this year. We all have loved ones who won't be here to share this season with us. My prayer is that all of us, even in our grieving, will find new sources of hope, new expressions of love.

Questions for Reflection

1. *Have you experienced holiday times that were difficult because of the previous loss of a family member? Describe the experience—how you felt and how you handled it.*

2. *How do you respond to the statement "A potent relationship exists between the depth of our grief for someone who has died and the depth of the love we shared with that person"? Does this give you a different perspective on grief?*

3. *What are some steps you need to take in order to cherish more fully the moments you have with members of your family while they are still here?*

TAKE A BREAK

"The sabbath was made for humankind, and not humankind for the Sabbath." (Mark 2:27)

Sabbath is a problem for many of us. I admit that it is for me. Sunday is, after all, a workday for clergy. It's a much bigger issue than what we do on Sunday, however. Whether or not stores are open isn't really a big factor, although the old blue laws did provide a measure of societal support for the notion that we do need to take a break from it all every now and then. What it's really about is our own willingness to let go of everything for which we feel a sense of responsibility. What it's really about is our own willingness to appear to be irresponsible for a while so we can take on the greater responsibility of care for ourselves, our relationships with those we love, and our relationship with God. That is why the space of sabbath is needed. It is a time to set aside the busyness of it all and to attend to what matters most.

Sabbath   *February 1998*

Every once in awhile I need to take a break. Sometimes the routine gets to be too much, the demands too many, the energy reserve too small. I just need to get away for a bit. It's something different from taking a vacation, for vacations have pressures and demands of their own. It's about stopping the routine and maybe just doing nothing for a while, maybe just being by myself or with others for a while.

One of my favorite musicals in my younger years was *Stop the World—I Want to Get Off*. I was young enough then not to understand how intense, even desperate, that cry can become at times. I was ignorant enough then not to understand that one of the keys to living a good, happy, and faithful life is never letting yourself get to the point of needing to utter such a cry.

I didn't know enough to realize that back then. In fact, it's taken me almost fifty years to understand it well enough to actually do something about it. But God has known about it all along. That's what the whole idea of sabbath is all about. It's a time of rest. It's intended to be a break from the routine. It's supposed to happen regularly enough that you never get to the point of desperation. Jesus said that the Sabbath was made for people, not people for the Sabbath. That sounds on the surface like a self-centered statement. But as usual, he knew what he was talking about.

We need the time of rest, the break from the routine. We need it to gather our energies for another day, to recharge our batteries. We need it also to remind ourselves that everything does not depend on our busyness, that the world can go on even if we stop for a while. Real sabbath rest depends on having enough humility to admit that we're not essential. It also depends on having enough faith to believe not only that the world is not in our hands, but also that it is in God's hands.

Why not think about taking a break from the routine? Do nothing for a while. I can almost guarantee that the world won't stop and your family will survive. In all likelihood, if you follow the necessary corporate personnel policies, your job will still be there when you get back. And, if Jesus had it right on this one—as we have every reason to believe he did—you and your family will be better for it.

Questions for Reflection

1. *Describe a time of real sabbath that you have experienced.*

2. *What keeps you from experiencing such times more regularly?*

3. *How can you help instill a sense of need for sabbath rest in your children? What implications might this have for the amount of their involvement in sports, dance, and other activities?*

Related Activity

Make specific plans for sabbath breaks in your routine. These can focus on enhancing your relationships with family members and with God. Remember: the essence of sabbath is *being* not *doing*. So plan to be with each other, not do with each other. The being may in fact involve doing, but put the emphasis where it belongs.

Section Seven

THE DAY-TO-DAY EVENTS OF FAMILY LIFE CAN BE ENRICHED IF WE *learn to do things together that celebrate who we are and acknowledge God's love and care for us. This section offers several conversations about what some of those things might be:*

+ **Play Together**
+ **Share the Richness of the Past**
+ **Find a Symbol**
+ **Create Rituals of Sharing**
+ **Celebrate Times of True Communion**

PLAY TOGETHER

Thus the heavens and the earth were finished, and all their multitude. And on the seventh day God finished the work that he had done, and he rested on the seventh day from all the work he had done. (Genesis 2:1-2)

Our days are full. We have work to do, errands to run. There's money to be made, bills to be paid. It can become overwhelming, especially if we also have young children who need tending. The responsibilities of being the adult presence in a family are great and serious. The problem is, however, that they can, if we let them, take all the fun out of life. Weighed down by responsibilities, life itself becomes heavy, and we begin to strain under the burden.

God didn't intend it that way. Children know that. They haven't lost the capacity for play, the ability to simply enjoy living and those they share life with. It's important for us as parents to play with children, so that we can share this significant part of their lives with them. But perhaps even more important is that we let children teach us again about the joy that can be experienced in play. At times, we just need to set aside our adult responsibilities and experience the simple joy of living. Genesis reminds us that even God gave up the busyness of creation in order to rest, to have a time of re-creation. That's what God intends for us, as well. When we do that, we not only help our children, we also help ourselves.

A Time to Play   *September 1995*

A few months ago, Ben and I spent some time at an arcade. Tossing all caution and every ounce of good sense I ever had to the wind, I decided that I would not obsessively count quarters, and would simply enjoy myself. Well, enjoy ourselves we did. Air hockey, skeeball, arcade games—on and on it went. But the thing that really got me that day was the two-seat racing machine. Ben and I each had a steering wheel and a car to drive in the race. We could race against each other as well as against additional cars. Quarter after quarter went down the slot as we laughed, cheered, and groaned our way through race after race. Sometimes he'd win; sometimes I would. What a time we had!

The image of us sitting there laughing together still has not left me. Something was special, very special, about that moment. There we were, father and son, almost teenager and almost "half-centurion," simply having fun together. The image hasn't left me, because on that day a lesson Ben has been trying to teach me for a long time finally sank in: *play is important.* Playing together is important to deep relationships. Learning to play is important to learning to live. Play is important, not because it is a way to escape (which, of course, it is), but because it is a way to re-create. It is a way to relieve the heaviness of our burdens. It is a way to reenergize ourselves for the challenges we face each day. It is a way of life that puts being ahead of doing, enjoying ahead of accomplishing. Ben wouldn't explain it that way; that's not the way a twelve-year-old thinks. But deep down inside, something tells him just how important playing is to his well-being and to mine. He is wise about this—much wiser than I am.

This idea, of course, isn't new to Ben. It's been around quite a long time. I think, in fact, that it originated with God. It was God, after all, who quit creating the world after six days and did something else instead. If the idea goes back that far and has such an influential proponent, I wonder why I (and so many others) struggle with it. I can't speak for the others, but I have a sense that the degree to which I feel free to play is inversely proportional to the degree to which I think everything depends on me. If I believe that it's all up to me to make it right or good or successful or comfortable or whatever, then there's virtually no chance that I am ever going to play. The burden of self-imposed responsibility is just too great for anything as frivolous as that. But it is a false burden, one that denies me some of the joy of life and the richness of relationship. It is a burden I need to let go of.

So, Ben, don't give up on your old man. Keep on asking me to go bowling and to the arcade and to play a game with you. With your help, I'll keep getting better and better at this playing thing, and in the process better and better at this living thing as well.

Questions for Reflection

1. *When was the last time your family laughed long and hard together?*

2. *Can you remember a recent time when one of your children asked you to play? What did you say? If you said no, what reason did you give?*

3. *What are your favorite memories of playing with other members of your family?*

4. *What "responsibilities" do you need to set aside in order to be able to play more freely?*

Related Activity

Plan a regular time together with a family member or members to do things that are fun. Celebrate these good times. Talk about them when they are over in order to hold their value in your thinking.

SHARE THE RICHNESS OF THE PAST

We will tell to the coming generation
the glorious deeds of the LORD, *and his might,*
and the wonders that he has done.

—*Psalm 78:4*

In this age of mobility it is easy to lose a sense of connectedness—with the past, with older generations. But every family has its history, an array of past experiences that make it what it is today. Some we are conscious of, others not. If we are conscious of more of them, we can have a greater appreciation for the struggles, triumphs, and day-to-day experiences of those in our family who came before us. From the perspective of faith this also helps us develop a deeper understanding of the ways in which God has been at work in the previous generations of our family. The psalmist proclaimed the need to do just that for the children of Israel—to tell of God's glorious deeds so that people would know all that God had done in and through the lives of those who had gone before them. The need for this is no less important for families. Remembering the past is a great way to celebrate both who we are and whose we are. It establishes the connectedness we need to live lives that are faithful both to our families and to God.

The Anniversary Quilt   *November 1992*

Sometimes it's difficult to remember why we have reason to be thankful. Our nation, indeed the entire world, seems oppressed by cynicism and negativism. We are in a recession that, before it is over, will have reshaped our economic landscape as much as a winter storm reshapes the beaches of the Jersey shore. Violence is on the increase; basic values, on the decrease. Stress and strain are up; peace and quiet, down.

In times such as these it's difficult to remember why we have reasons to be thankful. This is true for my family too, even though we're basically a pretty positive group of people. We look for the best and usually find it. We approach our problems as opportunities for change and growth, and they usually end up being that. But still, it's difficult some days to remember why we have reason be thankful. On days like that I think about the anniversary quilt.

For my parents' fiftieth wedding anniversary, each of the friends invited to their party received a square of cloth. We asked them to put something on it that symbolized their relationship with my parents and bring it with them. These squares became the basis for a marvelous time of sharing and are now sewn together into a quilt that hangs on their bedroom wall.

There's a wreath with "Friendship Is the Rarest Gift of All" written inside. It was done by a childhood friend of my mother. Years had passed since they had seen each other, until one day in 1948, shortly after moving into their new houses, they passed each other on the street while out walking their year-old children. So they became neighbors, babysitters, house watchers, and friends who have remained so for more than forty years.

There are embroidered bells and flowers from "Friends since 1936"—my father's college roommate and his wife. We shared vacations together, went through career changes and moves together. Through all the years and across all the miles they stayed in touch, good friends always, even—especially—when this old friend was diagnosed with Alzheimer's disease, and that long, inevitable, painful road had to be traveled.

There's a picture of a sailboat, with the caption "Watch out for that dagger board!" It refers to an event that happened some forty-five years ago but still brings gales of laughter to the eight good friends who watched as those instructions went unheeded.

There's a basket full of flowers from the then eight-year-old niece who was their flower girl. She too is older now; living in Arizona; children grown and married; loving, sharing, caring as her husband recovers from a stroke.

There's a needlepoint paint pallet, symbolizing years and years and years of painting lessons, laughter, sharing, aging, learning, growing. It started out as a way to escape from the captivity of young children by having something "adult" to do. But it grew to be so much more than that.

There's a square from the family. Bonnie, Jeff, Judy, Chris, and Ben—daughter, son, daughter-in-law, grandsons. Family.

There's great joy in that quilt, and also great sadness. But most of all, it has a richness of life—richness that comes from love, from friends and family sharing together all that life has to offer. The joy and sadness, the happiness and sorrow, blend together with a richness that can only be described as a gift. A gift of friend to friend, of husband to wife, of parents to children. A gift of God to all of us.

There are days when it's difficult to remember why we have reason to be thankful. On those days I think about the anniversary quilt. And once again I know.

Questions for Reflection

1. *Who are the people with whom you have had the longest friendships? What makes these friendships special to you?*

2. *How do you share the experiences of your parents' lives with your own children?*

3. *In what ways do you see these experiences as a gift from God, both for those who live them and for those who hear the stories about them?*

4. *If you were to create a quilt that told of the significant experiences of your family's life, what would the squares look like?*

5. *In what other ways can you pass along your understanding of family to future generations?*

Related Activity

Make a family quilt, either of paper or cloth, with squares that picture the key experiences of your life together. When it's finished, hang it in a place where everyone can see it often.

FIND A SYMBOL

When your children ask in time to come, "What do these stones mean to you?" then you shall tell them that the waters of the Jordan were cut off in front of the ark of the covenant of the LORD. . . . *So these stones shall be to the Israelites a memorial forever. (Joshua 4:6-7)*

In some ways, families are like nations. One of the continuing concerns of the people of Israel was how they and their children would remember what God had done for them. The ritual of the Passover was one way they helped insure this. They also used symbols. When the people crossed the Jordan River into the Promised Land, twelve stones were taken from the riverbed and erected there so that people would see them and remember what had happened, how God had provided for them. And in future years when their children and their children's children saw the stones they would ask, "Why are they there?" and the story could be told once again.

Symbols can be important for families too. They are concrete objects, linked to an experience. When we see the object, we are prompted to remember the experience and to tell the story to others. This remembering and telling allows the experience to continue to live within us, to continue to shape who we are and how we live together. Without the symbol the remembering would be more haphazard, the telling less often, the power to shape less profound. Sometimes we can name a symbol; sometimes we just claim it. However it comes to us, it adds richness to our life that we couldn't have without it.

The Gift of a Stone   *November 2000*

We bought our first house in 1978. We lived there for ten years, during which time both Chris and Ben were born. Because of that, it's a house full of important memories for us. It's the first place they remember. The place where they took their first steps, developed their first friendships, began their first years of schooling. It's also the place where Judy and I met the first challenges of being parents, wondering many times if we could possibly survive the ordeal . . . wondering as well if anything could be more awesome, more awe-inspiring. And there is also the gravel driveway.

It wasn't much, really—mainly a collection of small stones that were less than an inch in diameter. While we lived there, I did a good bit of traveling. Once, when Chris was about three, we were all standing at the end of the driveway as I was getting ready to get into the car to go to the airport. As Judy and I were talking, Chris picked up one of the small stones and gave it to me. Without thinking much about it, I stuck it in my coat pocket.

During the trip, however, every time I put my hand in that pocket, I felt the stone. And I would think about him, my family, and all they meant to me. Somehow, even miles away from home, I felt closer to them. I kept the stone in the coat pocket for as long as I had that job. Whenever I traveled, it was always there. I would touch it, clutch it, remember them, and somehow feel not quite so far away.

Now, that stone sits on my dresser and serves another purpose. I've looked at it often during these past months and discovered a different kind of power that it has. You see, Chris has been studying in China since the end of August and won't be home until just before Christmas. He is the one who is away, not me. The years since he gave me that stone have brought many other changes as well. He is no longer a curious three-year-old, but a young adult interested in the world and figuring out his role in it. He's a lot more independent now, too. The years ahead will undoubtedly bring more and longer times of being apart. I travel. He travels. Before long, he'll be living in some other part of the country—or the world.

But there will always be the stone—a simple little thing that will help me remember. Seeing it, touching it, will bring back memories of the day he gave it to me. It will lead me to reflect on all that has happened since that time. It will help me affirm the continuing richness of our relationship—all that he has meant to me and I to him. It will encourage me in the hope that no matter what changes the coming years bring, the richness of our family bond will always be there and always mean as much to us as it did that day in the driveway.

These concrete reminders of relationship are important. The stone in and of itself means very little. But Chris's gift, what he was trying to say by it, and the meaning it has acquired over the years make it a concrete representation of the life we have shared together. Seeing it, touching it, somehow makes it easier to remember and allows me to remember much more deeply.

I think that this is what Jesus had in mind at the Last Supper. It wasn't a stone he shared, but bread and wine. Still, they were and are concrete reminders of relationship—something that allows us to remember more deeply.

A stone. Bread and wine. Important symbols that point to a deeper, richer reality. Symbols like these are important for any relationship.

Questions for Reflection

1. *Look in your wallet or your purse. What concrete reminders of relationship does it contain? What other symbols of your family relationships are important to you?*

2. *What memories do these objects evoke for you?*

3. *Think about the objects that are around your house. Could they be "symbols waiting to happen"? How can you give them the meaning they deserve, so they in turn can help you remember and cherish more deeply?*

Related Activity

Be sensitive to the possibilities of symbols of your family life. These can't be forced, but we need to be sensitive to the potential for them to develop. In a family discussion, use some of the questions for reflection to probe the possibility of symbols that will have meaning for your family.

CREATE RITUALS OF SHARING
For as often as you eat this bread and drink the cup, you proclaim the Lord's death until he comes. (1 Corinthians 11:26)

Have you ever noticed how many greeting cards have a message that begins with something such as, "Although I don't often say how much I love you and how much you mean to me . . . "? The need for greeting cards to say what we want to say but don't affirms a great truth about living as a family. In the rush of living there is rarely the opportune time to share with each other about the things that matter most—how much we love each other, how much we mean to each other. Sure, we know that about each other already, but it's good to say so. Saying it is especially powerful if we can do it without help from greeting cards. One way to break the pattern of busyness that gets in the way of sharing is to create rituals—time to stop the routine, do something different, and share with each other. Weekly, monthly, even yearly rituals of sharing can have a profound affect on those who use them. They can provide continuity to life by designating specific times in which you gather, remember, celebrate, and cherish the things that are important to you.

In writing to the Corinthians, Paul reminded them of the power of the ritual of the Lord's Table. Each time they gathered there they remembered, but they also proclaimed who they believed Christ was, who they were, and what would happen. In the same way, rituals of sharing are times to remember what has happened and proclaim what will be within our families.

Thanksgiving French Fries   *November 1993*
It's funny how traditions get started. Two years ago on Thanksgiving Day we were sitting around my mother-in-law's apartment in Ocean City, New Jersey—a bit tired, a bit crowded, beginning to be overwhelmed by the smell of turkey cooking in the oven. Ben, then eight years old, and I decided to escape by taking a walk on the boardwalk. The walk led us eventually to the Chatterbox Restaurant to share a

plate of French fries. Last year we celebrated Thanksgiving at home, but when Ben and I drove my mother-in-law back to Ocean City on Saturday, we decided to top the day off with another walk on the boardwalk and French fries at the Chatterbox.

And so this year our plans for Thanksgiving Day were made to allow Ben and me our "time together." We'd get up early enough to drive to Ocean City so we could have our walk and French fries and still be ready to eat Thanksgiving dinner at two o'clock.

It's cold and windy that day, so the walk on the boardwalk is an abbreviated one—about a hundred yards! From there we make our way to the Chatterbox and slip into the very same booth we have sat in for the past two years. Our waitress arrives and we order: a Coke for Ben, a Diet Coke for me (even on Thanksgiving!), and a plate of French fries. We sit and talk. About the past two years and how this tradition got started. About school. About stuff.

The French fries arrive. We grab the ketchup bottle, shake a good bit out on the plate, and begin our dipping. We eat slowly. We talk slowly. We smile and laugh. Ben reminds me how last year, when we finished eating, I discovered I didn't have any money and he had to pay the bill. We laugh some more. We talk about next year and whether we'll be able to share our Chatterbox French fries again. Will we be in Ocean City? Might we make it sometime on Thanksgiving weekend to bring "Grams" home? We make a date. This is something we will do. It's become our time together, our very own Thanksgiving tradition.

And my mind races years ahead. When this ten-year-old is twenty, occupied with the experiences of his own, much more independent, life, will he still share Thanksgiving fries with me? When he's thirty and has a family of his own, his own kids who want their time with their dad, will he still share Thanksgiving fries with me? When he's forty, and I'm almost eighty, will there be fries for us to share, time together for us? I wonder, "Does he, as young as he is, realize what a precious moment this is we share together? Can he possibly understand?" And Ben gets up from his place on the other side of the booth, and comes around to sit beside me. He puts his arm around me and says, "Thanks, Dad. I'm glad we have our time together."

Questions for Reflection

1. *What family traditions have you developed that help you affirm the importance of your time together?*

2. *What regular events in the life of your family can you name as traditions so that they will continue to be honored?*

3. *In what ways are these traditions signs of God's love made real in the life of your family?*

Related Activity

Establish and name a family tradition. It should be based on something you already do and enjoy. It can be as simple as going out for ice cream together. Naming it will give it a higher level of meaning and lead to deeper appreciation of the impact it has on your life together.

CELEBRATE TIMES OF TRUE COMMUNION

*When he was at the table with them, he took bread,
blessed and broke it, and gave it to them. Then their eyes
were opened, and they recognized him. (Luke 24:30-31)*

It's easy to miss the great things God is up to in our lives. Too often we're like those disciples on the road to Emmaus, so caught up in our own concerns and conversations that we miss what's happening right in front of our eyes. Sometimes, like them, we're fortunate, and something happens to alert us to the reality we've been missing. It is, I think, possible to attune ourselves to these "somethings" so that we will notice them more readily. If we can do that, then our sense of God's presence and work in our lives will increase. The more we live in that sense, the more life becomes sacred and the people we share it with become holy. In the midst of commonplace, everyday events, we can find a connecting to another that is true communion and brings deep meaning and a renewed sense of the way God is at work in our lives.

Another Plate of French Fries   *November 1994*

Ben and I made it back to the Chatterbox restaurant in Ocean City again this Thanksgiving. That makes four years now that we've shared a plate of French fries there before our big Thanksgiving dinner at my mother-in-law's. It's a good time, a time of sharing between father and son. But this year it was also a bit scary. You see, these times have been so meaningful in the past that I couldn't help but wonder how this year's excursion could possibly live up to its reputation.

We talked about his newest interest, biking—the track he and some friends are building, the new things for his bike he hoped he'd get for Christmas. We talked about his report card and his hope that by next marking period the one B+ would become an A; how he was not upset at the one teacher who didn't give him an A, because he "probably didn't deserve it." We talked about the things that are different from last Thanksgiving: he's wearing glasses; he's in middle school; he's got a paper route.

We talked about the changes that have taken place in our lives during the past year. His grandparents sold their house in Rhode Island, so there will be no more family trips to the house I grew up in, for me to share those memories with them and to create some new, important memories in that old, important place. Aunt Helen, the only very old member of our family, died last spring, so there will be no more visits with her to cheer her up, to offer her something to look forward to, and to remember her in her struggle to come to terms with a life that was becoming increasingly difficult for her.

The French fries seemed to disappear faster this year than ever before. It was nothing special, really. We just talked, about the simple things, the everyday things, the important things that happen in life.

And then, just one French fry was left on the plate. Ben took it . . . broke it . . . and gave it to me.

True communion.

Questions for Reflection
1. *As you look back on your life, describe times in which you now recognize that God was at work in your relationships, but you did not notice then.*

2. What are the times and places in which you share together about the everyday events of living together in a family? In what ways do these offer you a sense of communion—with each other and with God?

3. What has God "broken and blessed" for your family?

Related Activity

Set aside a time each month to talk together about the things you've done with each other during the past weeks. Look for patterns of caring and sharing. Thank each other for these experiences.

APPENDIX

USING THIS BOOK WITH SMALL GROUPS

THE CONVERSATIONS OF THIS BOOK CAN BE GREATLY ENHANCED BY involving more people in them. If you have been able to do that, the following suggestions for group meetings will help you share together about your personal conversations during the week.

The first meeting plan is for an introductory session before you begin the daily work that the book suggests. The remaining plans are for each of the seven sections of the book. A commitment to meet once a week for eight weeks will provide a meaningful time of sharing and growing.

INTRODUCTORY SESSION

Plan to have light refreshments available as people arrive. If people aren't acquainted with one another, be certain to make introductions during this time.

When the group settles down, begin by asking, "What was it that led you to say yes to being part of this experience?" Allow time for people to share. Encourage those who might not have shared to do so by asking, "Is there anything else?" when the conversation dies down. Conclude by noting similarities and differences in reasons for participating, reminding the group that in the sharing that will take place in the weeks ahead a wide range of needs can be met.

Distribute copies of the book to group members who do not already have one. Invite the group to leaf through it. Take a few minutes for this. Briefly describe the basic structure of the book. It is divided into seven sections, one for each of the seven weeks you will be together. Each of the sections contains five "conversations" on issues involved in parenting. Encourage group members to do one conversation each day during the week, allowing twenty to thirty minutes for this. Ask them to record their answers to the questions for reflection, either in a notebook or in the book itself.

Have group members turn to the first conversation in Section One. Ask one person to read the Scripture passage and the introduction. Then ask someone else to read "A Scary Thing." As time allows, discuss responses to the questions. This will help model the approach of the conversations for group members, as well as begin the process of sharing with each other.

Explain that other groups of this type have found it helpful to have some common understandings that will govern their sharing. Guidelines that have proven helpful include:

+ honor the experience and perspective of each group member
+ maintain confidentiality by keeping all conversations within the group
+ place an emphasis on listening
+ make attendance and participation a priority

+ accept responsibility for yourself and for the care of other group members
+ share the talking time in group meetings as equally as possible

Discuss these guidelines as a group. Ask the group if they would like to add any further guidelines. Seek agreement on the ones that the group members will observe. Explain that these agreements form the covenant that is the basis of your life together as a group.

Clarify plans for next week's meeting.

Conclude with a prayer of blessing and encouragement, seeking God's guidance and openness to God's word in the week ahead.

SECTION ONE SHARING

After preliminary greeting and eating, bring the group together and ask, "How did it go?" Encourage them to share their experiences in doing the daily sessions. Were they able to do one each day? Did they find the time they needed to respond to the questions? In what ways did the conversations help them to see more clearly the importance of faith in parenting?

Ask, "What insight or story struck you most in this week's conversations?" Allow several people to share. Encourage others to reflect on their own response to the things that struck others.

Note that the book's introduction states that one of the things a church should be saying to parents is, "We know that parenting is one of the most important things you will do in life. We want to help you, so we are inviting you to deepen and enrich your relationship with Jesus Christ, because that, in and of itself, will make you a better parent." Then ask these questions: Based on your reflections this past week, how do you respond to that statement? In what ways do you think this book and this group may help you do that?

Ask group members for particular prayer concerns they may have, especially concerning their families and their role as parents. Conclude the session by spending time on these concerns and asking God's blessing on group members as they continue to work through the book during the coming week.

SECTION TWO SHARING

When group members have settled in, begin with words such as these: "This week's conversations were about important hopes to bring to our role as parents. We looked at five of these: cherish memories, nurture the experience of God, practice hushness, call forth gifts, and encourage standing alone. Which of these did you find most significant for yourself as a parent?" Encourage several group members to comment and others to respond to them.

Select from the following questions, or devise your own, to encourage continuing discussion:

+ Which story could you relate to most easily out of your own experience as a parent?
+ Was there any point at which you struggled with what the writer was talking about because you couldn't understand his point or because you disagreed with him?
+ Which of the five hopes do you think you realize best? Which do you struggle with?
+ How does calling forth the God-given gifts of our children shape our roles as parents? How have you done that with your children?
+ In the last conversation the writer talks about the importance of helping children "stand alone" for things that they believe in. Is this a quality that you try to nurture in your children? Why? How do you think this will help them live more faithfully both now and as they grow older?

Conclude the session with a time of prayer. Ask group members for both celebrations and concerns related to their families. Pray together, thanking God and asking for God's continuing blessing.

SECTION THREE SHARING

Begin the session by reminding the group that last week you focused on hopes we bring to our role as parents, and that this week the focus is on those things that we have little or no control over in life and in our families. Ask group members to list what they believe some of those things are.

Then ask which of the conversations provided them the most helpful perspective on dealing with those "uncontrollable things."

If this discussion hasn't led to group members referring to specific passages in the section, ask them to review it now and share a quotation that they found particularly helpful.

Use some of these sentence completions to encourage further discussion.

When I am faced with something in my family that I have little or no control over,

✦ my natural tendency is to . . .
✦ my greatest fear is . . .
✦ my prayer is . . .
✦ my first reaction is to . . .

For the closing prayer, offer to God the list of things we have little or no control over that the group developed in the first step. Ask God for strength of trust and depth of faith to deal with these in a faith-filled way that will strengthen your families.

SECTION FOUR SHARING

Begin the session by reminding the group that this is the first of two weeks in which the focus will be on some of the challenges you face as parents.

Ask, "What, so far, has been your greatest challenge as a parent?" After group members have shared, ask each one, "On a scale of one to ten, with ten being "great," how would you rate your handling of the challenge you shared?"

When group members have finished giving their ratings, ask, "Were there any insights in this week's work that would help you raise that rating? What were they? How would you use them?"

Note that many of these challenges are personal, rather than relational—about our own growth, rather than the way we relate to our children. Ask, "Why is our own continuing growth as people and as Christians so important to our effectiveness as parents?"

Ask group members to complete this sentence: "As I face the challenges involved in being a parent, the thing I need most is . . ."

Close with a prayer asking for God's presence in your lives as you face the challenges of being parents. Ask particularly for God to work in ways that will provide for the needs that group members have stated.

SECTION FIVE SHARING

Begin this session by asking group members to reflect on their experience so far in working through this book, both personally and as a group. What have they valued most? What has been most difficult? Is there something that can make the remaining weeks more beneficial to them? Explore these together. Make adjustments in the schedule or plans as needed.

Remind the group that this week continued the focus on meeting the challenges of parenting. Take a different approach to discussion this week by working through each of the conversations. As you do so, you might use each of the following questions to begin the discussion:

+ *Taking a Stand*: When have you felt the need, because of your faith convictions, to approach a situation with your children differently than do most other people? How have your children responded to that?
+ *Giving Thanks When the Going Gets Tough*: Do you think that Paul's counsel to "give thanks in all circumstances" is realistic even in the midst of difficult life situations?
+ *Letting Children Teach*: In what ways have your children taught you?
+ *Speaking Truth with Love and Laughter*: How do you deal as a family with the less positive aspects of a person?
+ *Relying on God's Forgiving Love*: Has a sense of God's forgiving love helped you move beyond failures you have had as a parent?

Ask group members to share about a particular challenge they are facing now as a parent. Allow time for description of the challenge(s). Without simply offering advice, work together to see if some of the insights of the past two weeks can apply to each situation.

Close with prayer, asking God's continuing power and peace in the midst of the challenges of family life. Encourage all group members to participate in the prayer.

SECTION SIX SHARING

Begin by asking if anyone has attempted to do one of the "related activities" suggested with some of the conversations. If so, ask them to share their experience with it. Note that in these last two weeks there will be more of these suggestions. Encourage group members to try one.

Remind the group that having dealt with things over which we have little or no control and then the challenges we face as parents, we move in these last two weeks to looking at more of the day-to-day routine of family life. As always, our focus is on seeking God's presence in the midst of our lives.

Note that the first two conversations deal with the very thin line between involvement and noninvolvement in our children's lives, between providing support and giving freedom, between nurturing and controlling. Use some of these questions to guide the discussion:

+ The writer indicates that this is an issue for parents almost from the point at which our children begin to walk, that it simply works itself out around different issues and in different ways at different ages. Do you agree? In what ways do you experience this tension with your children?
+ Do you have a natural tendency toward holding on or toward letting go in your relationship with your children?
+ Is there a difference in how fathers versus mothers approach this issue? Are sons handled differently than daughters are? How do such differences surface in your family?

Ask group members to reflect on the difficulty or ease with which they find time to take a break from the demands of parenting. Have they found ways to make it happen? What have been the benefits for them? If this is something that most group members find difficult, as many parents do, you might want to explore ways in which you can help each other in this effort.

Ask for specific concerns that group members would like to offer for prayer. Close the session with prayer for these concerns and for a sense of God's presence in the day-to-day routine of family life. Ask group members to share their prayers.

SECTION SEVEN SHARING

Begin the session by asking which of the stories in this week's conversations group members found most meaningful and helpful. Allow a time of conversation about these, and then ask, "What do they suggest to you about activities you can develop for your family?"

Ask the group to think back over your weeks together. Ask them to complete some or all of the follow sentences:

+ "The most significant learning of this experience has been . . . "
+ "The thing I have appreciated most about this group is . . . "
+ "Something I hope will be different in my family because of this experience is . . . "
+ "I hope that . . . "

Be prepared to discuss future possibilities for group members. Do they want to continue on some basis? Would some group members like to provide leadership for another group and encourage other parents to participate? Explore these or other options if there is interest.

Ask the group to join in a closing prayer of thanksgiving for the experience you have shared and for God's ongoing guidance as you continue to grow in faith and as parents.

INDEXES

STORIES

A Field of Dreams. 58
A Friend's Wedding. 28
A Scary Thing 2
A Special Day 31
A Time to Play. 125
Another Plate of French Fries 142
Another Year 67
Apple Pie Wonder 71
Coming Home Again. 110
Curse or Blessing 91
Daffodils or Peeling Paint ? 79
Getting Out of the Way. 107
Getting Wet 83
Grounded. 15
Happy Ending 62
Holiday Preparations 117
Intense Anticipation 50
It's a Different World. 46
Just Three Seconds. 11
Not Another Pavarotti. 36
On Uncertainty and Fear 54
Out of the Blue 114
Sabbath 121
Sometimes It Hurts 98
Stacking 95
Starting Over 102
Thanksgiving French Fries 139
The Anniversary Quilt. 129
The Gift of a Stone 134
The Independent 40
The Real Holiday Priority. 87
The Wonder of Baseball 24
The Wonder of Saying Yes 7
Truth in Packaging 74
Twenty-five Years 19

SCRIPTURES

Genesis
2:1-2 124
7:7 83

Leviticus
25:10 14

Joshua
4:6-7 133
24:15 40

Psalms
25:4-5 27
69:1-2 45
78:4 128
139:1-4 74

Proverbs
22:6 1

Ecclesiastes
4:6 31

Isaiah
40:3 10
43:19 49
55:8 106

Joel
2:28 94

Mark
2:27 120
4:40 53
8:34 6

Luke
24:30-31 140

John
8:32 98
10:10 66

Romans
8:28 57
12:2 86
12:3,9-10 19

1 Corinthians
11:26 138

Ephesians
2:8-9 114

Philippians
2:12-13 110
4:8 79

1 Thessalonians
1:2-3 117
5:16-18 90

2 Timothy
1:6 35

Hebrews
12:1-2 23

1 Peter
1:3 62
4:10 70

1 John
1:9 102

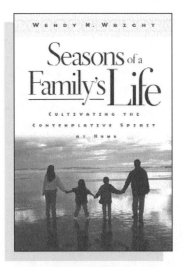

Seasons of a Family's Life
Cultivating the Contemplative Spirit at Home

Wendy M. Wright
$21.95 Hardcover
ISBN: 0787955795

"Wendy Wright has written a revelatory book about family life. So often taken for granted, so often discounted as drudgery, in her gentle, but skilled hands the life of the family is transformed into spiritual reality. As she probes the dish-washing, car-pooling, diaper-changing, curfew-setting reality of every day life she guides us to sacred ground."

—JAMES P. WIND, president, the Alban Institute

In *Seasons of a Family's Life*, highly-respected writer Wendy M. Wright offers a reflective, story-filled examination of the spiritual fabric of domestic life. It focuses on the cultivation of spiritual awareness amidst the ordinary drama of family life and challenges families to wrestle with the great religious questions which have always been a part of our human quest: Who in fact *am* I? What is a life well-led? What is most essential? What is my responsibility to others? How do I deal with evil? What constitutes the good?

Wright has a particular gift for combining a deep seriousness of purpose, a poetic use of language, and a great sense of humor. With this approach, she explores family life as a context for nurturing spiritual practices, providing parents with suggestions for developing contemplative practices in the home. Each chapter is a lesson in being attentive to the wonder of our experience in family, glimpsing the sacred amidst the chaos of our daily lives.

WENDY M. WRIGHT is a popular speaker at retreats, workshops, and conferences, and a professor of theology at Creighton University. Wright is a frequent contributor to *Weavings* and *Family Ministry,* and is the author of 11 other books. She and her husband live in Omaha, Nebraska, and are the parents of three young adult children.

[PRICE SUBJECT TO CHANGE]

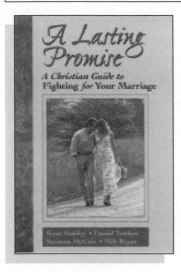

A Lasting Promise
A Christian Guide to Fighting for Your Marriage

Scott Stanley, Daniel Trathen, Savanna McCain, Milt Bryan
$17.00 Paper
ISBN: 0787939838

"I've been praying many years for people to discover from sound research why married couples separate and how to help them stay together in a loving way. I truly believe God has given us such a team in Scott Stanley and his colleagues. I not only give his book "two thumbs up," but I lift both my hands in thanksgiving to God for his work."

—GARY SMALLEY, author, *Making Love Last Forever*

This essential resource offers Christian couples a well-researched and proven method for dealing with conflicts and resolving problems in their marriage.

A Lasting Promise offers solutions to common problems—facing conflicts, problem-solving, improving communication, and dealing with core issues—within a religious framework. With the ultimate purpose of upholding the sanctity of marriage, the book is filled with stories that reflect the sacred teachings of the scripture. The strategies outlined can help Christian couples to improve communication, understand commitment, bring more fun into their relationship, and even enhance their sex life. This book will serve as an invaluable resource for all couples who want to honor and preserve the holy sacrament of their union.

SCOTT STANLEY is a marital researcher at the University of Denver and a recognized expert on marriage who is regularly featured in major print and broadcast media. He is coauthor of *Fighting for Your Marriage* (Jossey-Bass, 1994).

DANIEL TRATHEN is a psychologist, codirector of Southwest Counseling Associates in Colorado, and an associate professor of marriage and family therapy at Denver Seminary.

SAVANNA MCCAIN is a psychologist with Kaiser Permanente in Denver and is involved with applications of Christian PREP in churches, including mentoring models.

MILT BRYAN is director of The Center for Couple Training in Lakewood, Colorado, where he conducts Christian PREP workshops for couples.

[PRICE SUBJECT TO CHANGE]

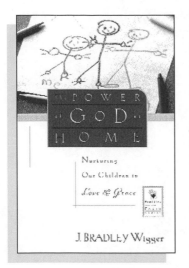

The Power of God at Home
Nurturing Our Children in Love and Grace

J. Bradley Wigger
$21.95 Hardcover
ISBN: 0787955884

"The Power of God at Home invites us to move beyond the mechanics of parenting and explore the spiritual practice of creating a family and home that nurtures faith and grounds identity. It weaves together essential ingredients (the biblical story, a realistic understanding of today's family, and concrete suggestions for how to begin) for helping parents and caring adults give our children the moral start they need in life. "

—MARIAN WRIGHT EDELMAN, president, the Children's Defense Fund

In *The Power of God at Home,* J. Bradley Wigger provides both a biblical model and practical suggestions for helping the entire family become aware of God's presence in everyday life. He reflects upon the powerful, formative influence of family life and considers what could happen if congregations understood families and not Sunday School classrooms to be the places where the deepest, most powerful learning takes place. He argues for the need to move away from seeing families as useless at spiritual formation and toward seeing them as potential bearers of God's grace and blessing and to equip them to play this role more consciously and effectively.

In a wise blend of storytelling, biblical exegesis, and practical suggestions for family activities, Wigger inspires us to renew our spiritual lives together as a family, welcoming God home.

J. BRADLEY WIGGER is a professor of Christian education, director of the Center of Congregations and Family Ministries at Louisville Presbyterian Seminary, and an editor of *Family Ministry*. He lives with his wife and two children in Louisville, Kentucky.

[PRICE SUBJECT TO CHANGE]